CHURCH
HEALED

Finding Healing: Navigating the Wounds of
Church Hurt with Faith and Forgiveness.

MERI DUARTE

ISBN: 979-8-89316-999-7 (paperback)
ISBN: 979-8-89316-980-5 (hardcover)
ISBN: 979-8-89316-998-0 (ebook)

JOURNAL PROMPTS
FREE GIFT

As you read this book of healing you might experience some memories or thoughts that will come up as you read my story of healing. I want to help you process and sit in your emotions as you read this book. I have included journal prompts to guide you and help you navigate any emotions or feelings that you may experience as you read.

You can download and use this free
resource for healing by visiting:
www.meriduarte.com/churchhealed

To my incredible husband.
Thank you for believing in me, encouraging me, supporting me,
and loving me the way you do.
I love you!

CONTENTS

INTRODUCTION

Something beautiful happens when we take time to rest: the Lord speaks to us and ignites passions and new desires in our hearts. I was enjoying the beautiful, beach weather of Playa Mujeres, Mexico, with my husband when the Lord placed a passion in my heart to write a book. I've never written a book, so this is all new and a bit scary for me. I am writing this out of obedience, believing that healing, forgiveness, and a new passion to serve the Lord in the local church will be ignited in your heart as you read my story and learn about my journey to healing.

I was enjoying my virgin piña colada and soaking my toes in warm white sand when the Lord said to me, I want you to write a book about your healing. A few months prior to this moment, we had gone through a huge loss in our family. We lost my brother-in-law and my father-in-law. I was coming out of a place of grieving and healing, so at first I thought that's what the Lord was asking me to write about. My heart was pounding in my chest and a million thoughts were going through my head. I felt His presence through the warm, refreshing wind of the beach; I felt His peace reassuring me that it was indeed my Father asking me to write a book.

Writing has always been a passion of mine. I had a little mommy blog and a photography blog for some time . . . but a book?! *Um, I don't know about that, Lord.* I sat there on that beach chair, wrestling with my thoughts, and asked God, "What can I possibly write about healing? Yes, I grieved, and yes, Lord, You healed me, but I am not sure I am the best expert on this grieving journey to write a whole book about it."

There have been two times in my life when I've heard God say shhh! to me, and this was one of those moments. He told me to shush because He was trying to speak to me and all I could do was ask Him and myself a thousand questions. So at that moment I got quiet, and I closed my eyes . . . and I saw it! The words "Church Hurt" with a slash across the word "Hurt" and the word "Healed" written underneath it. My eyes could not hold the amount of tears that were there. Of course I began to cry, as I always do. (I am such a crier.) And I'm currently crying as I write these words. Never in a billion years would I have ever thought that the Lord would ask me to share my story about the most painful and darkest times of my walk in the church.

CHAPTER 1

WELL, THAT HURT!

Y ou've picked up this book because you've been hurt by the church, and I wrote it because I was once there. For many years, I was bitter about the hurt I experienced within the church. It's never easy to pour your heart out and let people in during the dark and painful seasons of your life. But I am aware that this story is one God assigned for me to share so that it would bring glory to Him and so that many others would also find healing through it. I am confident that your story of healing will also impact many around you, even if the process right now seems like it's so far from healing. The process of healing is never easy, but it's always worth going through it. If you have felt like this process has been hard, I want to encourage you to continue to lean into the process that the Lord is taking you through this season. You're on the right track, my friend, and I am proud of you for already choosing the path to heal and remain. I know that reading this book will be part of your healing journey, in Jesus's name!

Even though the hurt is not your fault, it is your responsibility to decide what to do with the pain. It's your responsibility to forgive, to heal, to recognize that you are hurt, and to acknowledge that this pain is better surrendered at the Lord's feet.

WHAT IS CHURCH HURT?

First things first, let's address the elephant in the room. What is "church hurt"? Like any good millennial would, I googled it, and this is one of the first definitions that came up: "Church Hurt is a newer term referencing the pain, sadness, emotional scarring, or abuse experienced in a church context. Church Hurt can be inflicted, intentionally or unintentionally, by laity or religious leaders."[1]

Ouch! Sounds like the total opposite of what the church should be doing, right?

I actually grew up in church and never heard the term "church hurt." I was an adult the first time I heard this term. But how is church hurt even a thing? People don't usually use the phrase "job hurt" after encountering a conflict at work or having an issue with a coworker, or even after getting fired. They don't leave their jobs and never go back to work because they are "job hurt." And no one uses the term "school hurt" after getting bullied at school. So how is this "church hurt" phrase even a thing? I've come to realize that this term is thrown around more often than not because of

[1] Theos Team, "Church Hurt," Theos U., theosu.ca, accessed February 6, 2024, https://www.theosu.ca/theos-resource/church-hurt

Even though the hurt is not your fault, it is your responsibility to decide what to do with the pain. It's your responsibility to forgive, to heal, to recognize that you are hurt, and to acknowledge that this pain is better surrendered at the Lord's feet.

the expectation that churches should be full of perfect humans. Truth is, we have placed a high expectation on the church.

I've noticed some unhealthy patterns in the church that are actually hurting us more than bringing us together. Patterns like dishonor, dishonesty, pride, gossip, lack of compassion, lack of empathy, lack of integrity, and ultimately, lack of aligning the motives of our hearts to the Lord.

I hear stories and lived through those same stories about the way people have been hurt in the church. Stories of toxic leadership, misusing their power to bring guilt and shame to the congregation rather than love, grace and compassion. Judgmental behavior that can create an atmosphere of hostility and distrust, where members feel unsafe to share their struggles or doubts. Stories of when the leadership of the church may sometimes become overly focused on numbers, growth, or outward success, leading to unhealthy competition among members or even between different congregations. The most common one I hear is about the leaders or the pastors of the church not living what they are preaching. Seeing leaders and pastors fall in moral failure, or even lose their marriages and families for the sake of fame. Church hurt is something that has caused so many incredible people of God to fall and walk away from the Lord and the church. If it breaks our hearts, I can't even imagine what our heavenly Father feels when one of His sheep walks away and no one goes after it.

Unfortunately, we have allowed many of our past hurts to hurt others. Some of these church leaders are simply repeating behaviors they learned from other leaders, trust me, I was one of them. I knew that I needed to heal so that I would cut the domino effect and be a voice in the church to help others heal. If we don't heal we will also cause hurt within the church. It's important that we separate the church hurt from God's character. This hurt and

wounds were caused by broken people in the church, not by God. We unconsciously and automatically relate God to church, and so when people hurt us we blame it on God and walk away from Him.

It's important that we separate the church hurt from God's character.

But the good news here is that, yes, God is in the church, but He is not *the* church. Because if He was the church, then the church would be perfect, but it's not. The church is you and me! The church is composed of imperfect people, people who are still working through their character issues, life traumas, pride, and hurt. Does this make it okay for leaders or people in the church to hurt others? Absolutely not! But what is interesting, and I hope this brings some comfort to your heart, is that Jesus Himself experienced hurt within the church context. Do you remember all those Pharisees judging Jesus, questioning Him, and even dishonoring Him? The Pharisees were religious leaders, experts of the Law! You would think they would be the perfect people to teach others about God's ways. But Jesus called them hypocrites! I can only imagine how annoying it was to have people questioning Jesus, trying to go against what He was doing—God's will! But what did Jesus do? He replied with the truth, He responded with firm love, and He didn't let it take root in His heart. How beautiful, right? Imagine if we replied to those who hurt us the same way Jesus replied to the Pharisees and those who criticized Him. Even on the cross, Jesus said, "Father, forgive them, for they do not know what they are doing" (Luke 23:34). Jesus was in so much pain on that cross, He could not bear the weight of this world. So what did He do at that moment? He gave it to God. He cried out to Him!

Friend, I think it's time for us to realize that those people that hurt us aren't God! They aren't our good and faithful Father. They aren't Jesus—the one who died for us. They are humans just like you and me. No, it is not okay that they hurt us, but it is also not okay for us to put those church leaders or people on a pedestal, allowing their hurtful words and actions to consume the trajectory of our lives and the purpose we have in Him. The first two commandments God gave us were "You shall have no other gods before me" and "You shall not make for yourself an image in the form of anything in heaven above or on the earth beneath or in the waters below" (Exodus 20:3–4). These commandments did not only pertain to the Israelites, they are also meant for you and me, for His church. We have to be careful not to fall into dishonoring our leaders because the Lord calls us to honor, but we have to be very careful not to cross the line of honor to idolatry within the church context.

I have seen it time and time again, where church leaders or churchgoers, including myself, have idolized the pastor or the leader more than God. In my walk to healing, one of the main lessons I have learned is that I looked for the validation of pastors and leaders more than I actually sought God, which caused a lot of unnecessary stress in my walk with Him. There were many seasons in my life when my eyes were set on men and not on God. Many seasons where a leader's voice mattered more in my heart than

Friend, I think it's time for us to realize that those people that hurt us aren't God! They aren't our good and faithful Father. They aren't Jesus—the one who died for us.

God's voice. I have to admit, I caused myself a lot of the pain for not keeping my eyes on my heavenly Father.

We can't categorize God's character with the hurt we've experienced within the church context, or even in life. We are so quick to throw the blame of this fallen world to God, when in reality, from the beginning of times, God has just been trying to clean up this mess. God's character is compassionate, gracious, slow to anger, loyal, and faithful (Exodus 34:6). We need to bring our hearts back to HIM! Back to a Father who is faithful, who loves you, who is compassionate over your pain, and who wants to heal you.

Self-awareness is huge to your healing. It is important to be aware of those areas in your heart that are still offended and hurt. Even after years of being healed from the emotional hurt and spiritual abuse, I constantly ask the Holy Spirit to show me areas in my heart that are offended or hurt to ensure that my heart is pure despite people's motives, comments, or actions. I encourage you to invite the Holy Spirit in this moment to guide you through this area of your healing process.

We are so quick to throw the blame of this fallen world to God, when in reality, from the beginning of times, God has just been trying to clean up this mess.

A Father who is faithful, who loves you, who is compassionate over your pain, and who wants to heal you.

I hope this book brings healing to many who have experienced hurt within the church. I hope it encourages you to go back and serve in the local church to continue pursuing your God-given purpose and making a difference in your community. I invite you to journal any feelings and thoughts that come to mind as you read my story. I believe the Lord will use every word to bring you closer to a place of healing.

MY STORY

Disclaimer: I get really vulnerable. You're in for a ride, my friend . . .

There's power in vulnerability and authenticity, and you will see a lot of that in this book. I pray that through my story you are able to see the healing Jesus did in me. By no means is this part of the book to talk bad about any ministry, leader, or pastor in the church.

So buckle up, my friends. This is my story.

I was six years old the first time I ever went to church. I accepted Jesus at a kids' Sunday school classroom at a very small Baptist church. My parents didn't grow up in church, and in fact, both of my parents came from broken homes growing up. All my dad knew was witchcraft, and my mom just used God as an umbrella, meaning she only sought God when she needed to. So this world of churchgoers was a new thing to do as a family. It was new but we enjoyed it! It was refreshing to us. The Lord saved my parents' marriage, and we were grateful to now include God as the foundation of our family.

My desire to serve the Lord started at a young age. My mom got us involved in any type of church activity: the dance team, the kids' choir, the drama team, the kids' camps, and missing a Sunday was never an option. We loved the community we found within the church. The pastors were loving and caring, and the friends we made were genuine. I have great memories from that period of my life, and I am so grateful for it.

My parents did the best they could and always wanted, and still want, the best for us, so moving around from city to city, and even to different countries, was part of my childhood. Moving around so much meant changing schools and churches every year. We didn't have much stability, but it did get me out of my comfort zone to make new friends, and maybe that's why I am such an extrovert now. It allowed me to attend different churches and grow up seeing different types of denominations and cultures.

I remember so vividly the day my dad woke up and said we were moving to New York. I had been raised in Costa Rica and that was all I knew. I was twelve years old, but for some reason I wasn't surprised we were moving once again. We knew he just wanted the best for us, and leaving Costa Rica seemed the right choice since we had lost everything and needed a way out.

We moved to New York and once again hopped around to a few different churches. I remember walking into one where the pastors were so sweet. At the end of the service, one of the leaders pulled my parents aside and asked that my mom, my sister, and I wear skirts next time we attended since pants were not allowed in the church. They were so kind with their words, and I am sure they meant well, but it was very confusing for me. What was wrong with what I was wearing? Why couldn't we worship Jesus wearing pants? It was a bit of a culture shock for me because, in my years of going to church, I had never experienced this. But it stirred up curiosity in me to read the Word and educate myself on this topic at such a young age. I discovered the importance of knowing the cultural background behind a Bible verse.

We were just learning English and adjusting to a new culture, new school system, new friends, new way of living, and even the weather was extremely different. As we continued to visit churches for months, we finally found the one for us! This church had everything we were looking for (and we were allowed to wear pants!). El Remanente Fiel was a small, Pentecostal church, different from our Baptist background, but it was a nice chapter in our lives, and we grew closer to the Lord as a family. While we were there, I joined the youth group and the worship and dance team; I experienced my first Christian concerts; I was baptized with the Holy Spirit; and that's where I met my eventual husband. I was thirteen years old and he was fifteen when we met at a youth service. We later found out that we went to the same school, and soon after that we became best friends.

My family and I were at that church for about four years, when out of nowhere my dad once again had an idea: we needed to move to Miami, Florida. My dad just loved the adventure, I was not happy about it, especially because this time around I was a little older, I had built some pretty awesome friendships, I loved my drummer boyfriend, and I did not want to move again and start all over. I was tired of it. But six months later, we moved.

I remember the drive from Buffalo, New York to Miami, Florida. It felt eternal and I was so depressed, which made the drive even worse. I did not understand why my dad was moving us again when we were perfectly fine in New York. Over the years I have seen the story unfold and I am grateful we moved, but teenager me was not happy about it. Especially because I had to break up with my boyfriend. I wanted to get out of the car and run off, but I didn't. My Nicaraguan mom would have probably left me in the middle of the highway.

When we left for Miami, I was about fifteen years old. Once again, I was shocked by the culture change from New York to Miami. Not only was the actual city a huge change but so was our new home church. Remember, I had come from a very small Pentecostal church. We all knew each other: the pastor was my dad's friend, we were all a family, we had summer picnics, and everything was so cozy, or at least that's how it made me feel.

Well, not our new church. Our new church was a BIG, BIG megachurch. Nothing wrong with megachurches, but it was just different from what I was used to. I felt so tiny, and I definitely missed my friends and that cozy feeling. But this was a new beginning, and I had to adjust and find my way to start serving Jesus again.

I remember we were in a Sunday service when the dancers went to the altar during worship and I could not focus on worshiping because I was just so amazed by the dance team. I immediately fell in love with the idea of being part of their dance team and once again meeting new people. A couple weeks after attending, I tried out for the dance team and made it! The most epic moment of my life, or at least that's what I thought. Soon after that I became a leader in the youth group and was super involved in the church. Little by little my entire life became consumed by it. I thought "seeking the kingdom of God first" meant being at church twenty-four seven. This is where my resentment toward ministry began. My entire life was being consumed by being at church all the time. I was told I couldn't have plans outside of the church. I began to miss out on important family events because it was mandatory that I was at church. I was told that if I did anything outside of the church, then I was falling in disobedience, clearly not true.

I was there all the time, so obviously promotion came quickly. On the outside it was like, *Dang, girl, you're only seventeen and look at you with this big influence in this big church.* But in reality, I was so empty. I only prayed when I was at church, and then I would go back to school and try to fit in while also being the "Christian girl." Truly, going to church was something that I was just part of and *had* to do because that's what I grew up doing.

During this season, I experienced something that deeply impacted me. One of the leaders whom I absolutely loved and had served with for years was asked to leave the church. She had gone with another friend from church to get a tattoo, and when some of the leaders found out, they removed her from all leadership roles and asked her to leave the church because they deemed it a moral failure. I am aware that not all of us share the same thoughts regarding tattoos. But to kick someone out of the church for getting a tattoo? I was so confused, hurt, sad, and disappointed. If we are the church, why are we kicking people out as if the church was only for the people that look and think like us?

I was a really naive teenager with a lack of wisdom and no good leadership guidance. I graduated high school, felt convicted about the way I was behaving, the language I was using, the toxic relationships I had. That's when I repented and decided to follow Jesus wholeheartedly. I had an encounter with God at a conference in which God told me to remain obedient and to do His will, and so I did.

Well, during that time the Lord moved pretty quickly in my life. I started college, got a full-time job, and started to seek God first. Later on that year my cute drummer boyfriend from New York moved to Florida! We reconnected and began a friendship. When we started dating again, he was in another city about four hours away from me, and so one of us had to move when the time came to get married. We were both serving in the church, praying together, and really putting the Lord in the center of our lives and relationship. I have to be honest and say that even though I was still serving in the church, my motives were not in the right place; my heart was full of pride, and at times I only did it for the recognition. About two years later we got married! I moved to the city where he lived and started attending and serving at the church he was at. The most impactful part of my hurt came from this point of my life.

My husband and I became heavily involved at church. My husband, Martin, is a jack-of-all-trades; this man does it all! So that meant he served on just about every team: worship, production, church cleaning, new believers, discipleship classes, youth, and even preaching sometimes. I immediately became the dance leader and began to serve on just about every team as well. We were pretty much everywhere, doing everything. Unfortunately, we were too young to understand the power of boundaries. But also "boundaries" was a word we never had been taught. Our roles at the church always felt uncertain whenever we needed a break or tried to set boundaries. One incident in particular really affected me. Martin and I sat down with our pastors to discuss my request for some time off from my leadership responsibilities, so I could focus on my last semester of college. But things quickly turned sour. The pastor's wife threatened to remove my title in the church, remove all the leaders under me and disband the dance team if I took any time off. Martin, being the supportive husband he is, intervened, questioning why such severe consequences were necessary. After all, I wasn't doing anything wrong; I simply needed to prioritize my education over church commitments for a while. That's when tensions escalated. The pastor slammed his hand on the table, stood up, and yelled at us not to challenge their authority. We remained silent, we did not feel safe to express ourselves and the worst part was we did not have anyone else to talk to about this situation. We felt alone, broken, and so confused. During that season, we operated under fear rather than love. I have forgiven them, and I no longer feel shame when sharing this story. However, the impact endured for years, leaving a lingering sense of fear toward church authorities. For a long time, I believed I didn't deserve to be a leader if I wasn't willing to sacrifice aspects of my personal life for the sake of the church.

Sadly, we didn't have a good example in the church of what a healthy marriage looked like. We quickly moved up in hierarchy, and the more we moved up, the more we were exposed to lack of integrity, leadership neglect, dishonor, disrespect, and spiritual, emotional, and verbal abuse. When moral failures occurred within the pastors of the church, instead of exposing the sin, and helping the church get healthy, we were told to keep quiet.

At this point Martin and I were so broken that we were bleeding on the people God had entrusted us with. So before you think I was only a victim of the hurt, let me tell you, I was so blinded by my pain, open wounds, and pride. I had no idea how much hurt I was causing in the church myself. Hurt people, hurt people, and I was so numb to the hurt and humiliation that hurting others was just part of my leadership style in the church. I would put the same pressure that was put on me. I would scream at people, mistreat them, gossip about them, and not love them or lead them how God asked me to. We were so confused, hurt, and lost. Is this what God meant for the church to look like?

We served with other married couples in the same predicament as us: newly married, barely making it financially, leading out of fear, and in all honesty, just trying to receive validation from our pastors. But somehow through it all, Martin and I stayed strong together. We know for sure that God protected our marriage. Every time I think or talk about this season in my life, I think about God's sovereignty. How beautiful He is to protect our marriage, that even though we felt alone and in such a dark season of confusion, He still covered us in the shadows of His wings to fulfill His will over our marriage.

THERE'S STILL HOPE

My heart is filled with so much compassion and empathy to know there are still so many people going through this in the church, feeling broken, abused, neglected, and alone. Some now have even walked away from their purpose because of the hurt. I pray that the Holy Spirit uses this book to bring you a step closer to healing, give you hope, and allow you to fall in love with your first love again: Jesus! I pray by the end of this book, the Lord renews your passion to serve Him, seek Him, and abide in Him.

Maybe you can relate to a similar hurt within the church. Maybe what you have gone through or what you're currently going through is worse than the things I have experienced, or maybe you have been the reason why people have left the church. Don't worry, no judgment here—I was the reason why so many people left the church too. I have repented, He has forgiven me, and I have even reconnected with those I once hurt. Whether you were a victim or the one who caused the pain, there is hope, healing, and forgiveness for you too. I encourage you to take your first step today toward healing! If He healed me, He can heal you!

God does not want you to walk through this process alone. He desires for you to come to Him with your raw and vulnerable thoughts and emotions. Talking to God is crucial in your healing journey. Therefore, I have included prayers at the end of every chapter to assist you in navigating the feelings and emotions that arise as you read. I encourage you to vocalize these prayers, journal your emotions, and seek guidance from a counselor if necessary. Now that you are aware of some of the hurt I experienced, let us embark together on the journey of healing.

Dear heavenly Father,

Thank You, Father, for this moment. Thank You for the healing that You are already doing in my heart. Father, I recognize that I have been hurt by the church, not by You. In this moment I ask for forgiveness for holding all those leaders, people, and pastors to a standard that was not godly. I pray that You would help me to see those who have hurt me as You see them. Help me navigate through those emotions as I continue to read this book and remember the hurt. I recognize that my eyes were not set on You entirely. I recognize that I have let the hurt affect the way I see You, God. I recognize that the hurt that others have caused has affected the way that I serve You and love others. I accept Your forgiveness, I accept Your grace, and I accept Your love and mercy. Thank You, Father, for this season of healing. In Jesus's name, amen.

JOURNAL & REFLECT

- As I was reading this chapter, did any memories come up that I need to surrender to the Lord?
- Any stories that I need to mull over and process with the Holy Spirit or a professional counselor?
- In what ways have I allowed the hurt I've experienced within the church to negatively affect my relationship with the Lord?
- In what ways has the hurt I've experienced affected others?

CHAPTER 2

THE HARD PART

For a few years now I've considered myself a plant mom, but I wouldn't say I am the best plant mom. I have to admit I've killed more plants than what's probably legal at this point. I couldn't understand why some of my plants were dying, I was watering them, giving them a proper amount of sun, yet some weren't thriving or even surviving. I began to do my research and realized that I was missing a huge part of keeping my plants healthy, alive, and growing. Not only did I have to feed it some fertilizer, I also had to trim and prune the leaves that were yellow or dead. Our spiritual walk with God is very similar to keeping a plant alive. Not only do we have to keep a life of prayer, intentional time in the Word, but as well being able to be pruned and trimmed.

This chapter might be a little hard for you, as it was for me to understand what the Lord was doing in my heart to heal me. But I encourage you to keep reading. My friend, this is for YOU! For your heart, for your healing, for your process, and for your own good. So stay with me a bit. Just breathe as you read and give space for the Holy Spirit to encounter you right where you are. Give Him the scalpel and let Him perform an open heart surgery as you read this chapter. I encourage you to take a moment and give space for the Holy Spirit to embrace you and heal you as you read these words.

PRUNING

Friday mornings are my favorite; it is the only day of the week that I get to sleep in a little and feel the warm sunshine coming through the wide windows in our master bedroom. It reminds me of the miracle of every morning. It reminds me of His faithful love toward me. It's the only day I get to stay in bed in my cozy white sheets and read the Word, pray, and worship without the rush of getting the kids ready for school, making breakfast, working out, and doing everything else that needs to be done on any other weekday.

I was enjoying the slowness of my Friday morning with my fresh white bed sheets, some freshly squeezed orange juice and the warm sunlight coming through the windows of my bedroom, when the Lord said to me, "Remain." In that very moment the Holy Spirit led me to John 15.

I read through these verses:

> *I am the true vine, and my Father is the gardener. He cuts off every branch in me that bears no fruit, while every branch that does bear fruit he prunes so that it will be even more fruitful. You are already clean because of the word I have spoken to you. Remain in me, as I also remain in you. No branch can bear fruit by itself; it must remain in the vine. Neither can you bear fruit unless you remain in me* (vv. 1–4).

I was meditating on these verses when, at that very moment, the song "Tend" by Bethel Music came up on my worship playlist. The song is about God carefully and gently cutting areas of our lives that aren't pleasing to Him.

The Lord was clearly speaking to me. At that moment I just froze, and the Holy Spirit said to me, "Get ready for some pruning, but I need you to remain when the pruning gets hard and painful, because I will dig deep. I need you to remember to remain in Me!"

I journaled about that moment. I can't say I wasn't afraid or I wasn't wondering what this would look like. It was the end of 2022, and "remain" was my word for 2023. I never had a

"Remain and trust me."

specific word for the year, mainly because I never felt like God gave me one. I also didn't go out of my way to look for one. But this time, I had a word. I can't say that I loved that because it did make me wonder, What in my life is going to happen that the Lord is asking me to remain? What does this pruning mean? I had a million questions, but again I felt the Holy Spirit telling me, "Remain and trust me."

Next to the verses in John 15, I wrote in my Bible:

> *Father, cut every branch of my life that bears no fruit. Let every part of my life be fruitful, Lord. Help me remain in You. Bear much fruit through me. What You love can stay and grow. Help me love others, as You love me. Don't let my heart be troubled and afraid, let Your peace remain in my heart.*

Can I be super honest? I was so in the spirit at the moment I wrote that because I had no idea of the amount of pruning He was about to do. I had no idea of the amount of uprooting I had just given Him permission to do or of all the branches He wanted to cut. I had no idea that He would take His sweet time pruning my heart. And I had no idea of the number of humbling moments I was about to encounter or the number of conversations that were ahead of me, in which I would just need to stay quiet.

But God never misses a beat. He wanted to make sure I wasn't caught off guard. I've been caught off guard by Him before. But He loves me so much that He knew He needed to give me a heads-up. He knew what was ahead of me could have taken me out of the game if I did not remain in Him! So He needed to remind me to remain.

A year after that moment, I understood why He had asked me to remain. I was about to walk into a season that would bring lots of triggers to the church hurt I had worked so hard to heal for the past five years. I was about to experience a lot of criticism. I was about to walk into a season where I would see people in ministry that I loved falling into moral failure and where people were going to tell lies about me. I was about to experience dishonor, humiliation, betrayal, and misunderstandings (even by me just saying hello). A lot of changes in the church were not going to make sense. I was going to be humbled, and I was about to step into a season where I felt like my voice did not matter.

I was walking into a year of silence, understanding that I was not to defend myself. A season where I would be told I have the skills but not the authority. I was about to walk into a season that as much as I wanted to run away from, I couldn't. A year where the drives to church on Sunday mornings felt more like a cry for help because of my frustration. A season where I felt like I no longer had someone to defend me and acknowledge the great leader that God had created in me. A season where I felt forgotten and where frustration was the new normal. A season where I would be asking God, "Is this still a safe place, Lord?"

Father, cut every branch of my life that bears no fruit. Let every part of my life be fruitful, Lord. Help me remain in You. Bear much fruit through me. What You love can stay and grow. Help me love others, as You love me. Don't let my heart be troubled and afraid, let Your peace remain in my heart.

This was the year I learned how to see God as my FATHER! And where my loving and heavenly Father was going to lead me at His own pace. Many times He would tell me, "They aren't doing this to you. I am allowing this for you." Where His correction would embrace me and love me. Truth is, the many reasons I had to just quit and walk away from the church and ministry were valid. But no reason was greater than the one reason to remain: Jesus!

Through this season, or more like a whole year of pruning, I have learned something about God's timing: the Lord likes to take His time. Not because He likes to make us wait, but because things that are rushed, don't last. We don't value things that are quickly obtained as much as those that take time to grow. We appreciate them more, and we don't neglect the process.

> **Truth is, the many reasons I had to just quit and walk away from the church and ministry were valid. But no reason was greater than the one reason to remain: Jesus!**

I often think about how God could have snapped His fingers and created this entire universe in just a few minutes, because He is God and He can! He is almighty and all powerful. But He didn't do that; He took His time. Day by day, He created something new. Day by day, He spoke one thing at a time, taking His perfect and sweet time. God lives outside of human time. He does not rush anything. God wanted to take His time with me this year. He wanted me to feel the process of the pruning. And during the process, God wanted me to lean in and remain. He wanted me to learn more about finding and growing deep roots in Him—not in being a pastor, a leader, in a certain position, in a career, in a church, or even in my family. He wanted me to see past the imperfections of others and fix my eyes on Him.

I gave Him permission to cut the branches that were overgrown, the branches that were not allowing me to find my identity as a child of God. I gave Him permission to humble me, to put a mirror in front of me so I could see the ugly parts of my character that weren't bearing fruit in Him.

Pruning means that the Lord will cut off branches that do not bear fruit. Pruning comes with growing pains, humbling moments, and being in situations where you need to stay quiet. He will use the church, people, to mold us to His perfect design.

I could write about all the wonderful areas of who I am and not let you in the ugly parts of my character, but why would that matter if it does not bring glory to God? You see, I now understand that the ugly parts of me that He has now transformed into humbleness, patience, kindness, compassion, empathy, and gentleness are all for His glory, not mine. They're for me to walk as a testimony of healing and transformation. This is about how He can continue to glorify Himself through my life, my imperfections, and my weaknesses. It is not about how perfect and put together I look in front of a church or social media or other people. This is about the transformation that He has done in me to bring glory and praise to His name.

This book is not another tool to bash the church. This book is not about the people who hurt you. I believe God wants to use this book to let you know that the Lord is using what you've been through to work in your heart and be a testimony to bring others to healing. The Lord did not do this *to* you. He did this *for* you! Whether others were wrong and they offended you or hurt you, the Lord wants you to lean in and

> **The Lord did not do this to you. He did this for you!**

ask, What is this for? He will answer that question because the truth is that there's purpose in the process and in the pain.

I challenge you to identify what areas in your life need more of Him? What areas in your heart need His pruning? What lessons is He teaching you in the process?

REMOVING THE UNFORGIVENESS

For years I drank the poison of unforgiveness. The side effects were bitterness, regret, grudges, emotional stress, lack of trust in others, and lack of empathy and grace for others and myself. *It's not fair that someone hurt me in the church! It's not okay the way they spoke to me and made me feel. It's not okay that they took advantage of their position and mistreated me verbally and emotionally. They are wrong! They need to apologize! God needs to punish them! I'm never going to let anyone treat me like that ever again! How do they call themselves pastors when they never cared for me as a person?*

Those were the words of a broken girl who desperately needed to forgive. Those (and more) were the thoughts I had in my heart for years. Unforgiveness was a cancer that was slowly killing me. It penetrated every single one of my organs, immobilizing me from moving forward in my walk with the Lord. Immobilizing me from seeking and finding healing. It was not allowing me to walk in the perfect will of God. I had created many walls around my heart; no one was allowed in except my husband, but only because he is the most amazing person on earth. But I was wrong—so wrong! That's not how God wants me or you to live our lives.

RECOGNIZING THE OFFENSE

Growing up in church hearing sermons about forgiveness was not out of the norm. It was preached about often and always the topic for the salvation call. I knew forgiveness was always the right thing to do, but that did not mean I was forgiving others how God wanted me to.

Years ago I joined a small group. For an entire week we focused on the topic of forgiveness. Let me just tell you, it was not the week for me. I was not ready to forgive, and I did not want to hear it. But the Lord said, "Meri, ready or not, you need to forgive." That specific week the Lord wrecked me, healed me, loved me, and pulled me in closer. The book we were reading said this:

> **The root of unforgiveness is offense.**

Offense is the bait that the enemy uses to lure us into bondage. When we become offended we become unyielding. Think about a city surrounded by walls. The wall's purpose is to protect the city. We use this same thinking to protect ourselves, placing walls around our hearts. People may have hurt us once, but we will not allow them to do it again. But what works for a city of stone does not necessarily work in the same way for the heart of flesh and blood. Walls may keep out of the bad stuff, but they also keep out the good. With walls around our hearts, we not only protect ourselves from pain and rejection but from experiencing love and life-giving relationships. We think it is up to us to protect our hearts, but the truth is, God never meant for this to be our responsibility, it is His.[2]

The root of unforgiveness is offense. The enemy walks around depositing seeds of offense into our hearts. He finds any small open door to creep into and lets that offense grow into unforgiveness. Sometimes it's just a thought, and sometimes it's the

---

[2] Freedom Book p.78

actions of others that might rub us wrong. Whether the offense is tiny or large, if we allow it to penetrate our hearts, it will create great damage.

The offense in my heart had created walls—not drywall walls, strong brick walls! Walls that were hurting me. I had become a prisoner of my own offense and nothing could set me free, except my own willingness to

Forgiveness also does not mean "forgive and forget".

forgive. You see, I had the wrong idea of forgiveness. I thought forgiveness would make me weak. I thought it meant that what I had gone through did not matter. I thought forgiveness meant forgetting everything that had happened and automatically putting myself in a vulnerable state to allow others to hurt me again.

Forgiving someone does not minimize the offense. But choosing to forgive means letting go of the offense that is robbing us from living in true freedom. Forgiveness also does not mean "forgive and forget," and that is why many are still in the bondage of unforgiveness. When we forgive, we will probably still remember some of the things others did to us, but we will no longer allow that hurtful experience to relive in our hearts, memories, and emotions.

The truth is that the enemy will always use offense to create division, hurt, and hate within the body of Christ. Our hearts need to be proactive to the schemes and plans of the enemy. The Bible tells us that we have all "sinned and fall short of the glory of God" (Romans 3:23). That means we are all sinners. We are not perfect either, and when we recognize our own imperfections, that we are as much sinners as the person who offended us, it allows our hearts to let go of the offense.

Our hearts need to be proactive to the schemes and plans of the enemy.

We become proactive to not allow offense into our hearts by recognizing that the devil is our enemy, not our brothers and sisters in the faith. The enemy will use our humanity to offend and be offended, but the Word of the Lord tells us to be alert and sober in mind because the enemy is looking for someone to devour (1 Peter 5:8). The enemy knows the purpose and calling you carry, and offense is his way of being proactive for you not to walk in God's perfect will.

Lastly, when we root ourselves in God's love, nothing can move us. No evil can penetrate our hearts. Our hearts need to be so devoted and focused on Him, that even if the enemy uses anything to try to offend us, we know that we have a faithful Father who loves us and cares for us (1 Peter 5:7).

When we allow ourselves to be loved and embraced by our heavenly Father, it creates a protection around our hearts that allows us to see the good in others and not be easily offended.

> **When we root ourselves in God's love, nothing can move us.**

FINDING FORGIVENESS

Forgiveness is generally not our first response or desire because it requires sacrifice. In order for us to be forgiven, there had to be a sacrifice, and that was Jesus's blood on the cross. Forgiving those who have hurt us is walking in obedience and being a true living sacrifice. Did you realize that forgiveness is also worship to the Lord? I

> **Forgiving those who have hurt us is walking in obedience and being a true living sacrifice.**

never really saw forgiveness as a form of worship until I understood the beautiful aroma it brings to the Lord when we live in harmony with one another. I personally struggled with unforgiveness because I did not completely comprehend that God had forgiven me first. He forgave me for hurting others in the church too. He forgave me for once being that toxic leader myself. He has not only forgiven me for my past but also for my future sins. When we repent, God makes the choice to forgive us too. The relationship the Lord wants to have with us is the ultimate example of the relationships we need to have with one another.

God understands us. He came to earth so that we wouldn't have the excuse that He doesn't understand. He became human and came to earth to experience betrayal, offense, and hurt. He came to this earth so that we would feel understood and He could empathize with our pain. Jesus went through these trials himself. He was humiliated and disgraced. He was betrayed by Judas, falsely accused, and rejected by Peter and others that He loved and poured into. Jesus was abused, physically beaten, tortured, cursed, and crucified. Jesus is the ultimate example of how we need to respond when others hurt us, humiliate us, betray us, and accuse us.

The truth is, it's hard to forgive. That's because we are not supposed to do it in our own strength. Even Jesus at the cross said, "Father, forgive them, for they do not know what they are doing" (Luke 23:34). This was Jesus's cry for help. Jesus presumed the best intentions in these individuals, believing that their actions stemmed from ignorance

Jesus is the ultimate example of how we need to respond when others hurt us, humiliate us, betray us, and accuse us.

rather than malice. Jesus was asking the Father to intervene in the pain. When we are hurting, we can cry out to our Father too. Because with God, everything is possible, and if we invite Him into our pain, He will carry us through it.

My process of forgiveness toward those who hurt me within the church context was not a one-prayer done deal. It was hundreds of prayers. Why not one and done? Because it was a daily commitment to forgive. It was weeks and months of constantly dying to my bitterness, anger, and rage. Every time I felt it come up, I closed the door on it by praying. I was not going to let the memories of what they did to me open the door again for unforgiveness. Instead of asking God to help me forget what they had done to me, I chose to pray so the Lord would help me remember why I needed to forgive.

> **When we are hurting, we can cry out to our Father too. Because with God, everything is possible, and if we invite Him into our pain, He will carry us through it.**

Get rid of all bitterness, rage and anger, brawling and slander, along with every form of malice. Be kind and compassionate to one another, forgiving each other, just as in Christ God forgave you (Ephesians 4:31–32).

The apostle Paul says to get rid all of it. To get rid of something means to throw it out. He is not telling us to not feel it or that we'll never feel it. We will feel these emotions because we are humans, but we have to get rid of them. We cannot keep them in our hearts.

I think of daily forgiveness as us becoming minimalists when it comes to the junk in our hearts. When I am cleaning, I often say, "When in doubt, throw it out." It's an old phrase I learned from a coworker when I was a teacher. I have applied this very catchy phrase not only to my spring cleanings but also to my heart. When I find those extra things in my heart that don't pertain to love, compassion, forgiveness, patience, joy, peace, kindness, or goodness, I throw them out.

The most practical way you can do this is by asking the Lord to allow you to be aware of those areas in your heart that are far away from Him. Ask the Lord to help you remember any unforgiveness that is in your heart, even past hurt. Sit in solitude with Him and allow Him to reveal those hidden areas of your heart to be encountered by His grace, love, and forgiveness. Once you start to remember, write down names and situations that have caused offense and pain in your heart. I encourage you to ask the Holy Spirit to give you that bravery to let go of the pain, hurt, and offense caused by those in the church.

Sit in solitude with Him and allow Him to reveal those hidden areas of your heart to be encountered by His grace, love, and forgiveness.

Pray:

Dear heavenly Father,

Thank You for Your daily forgiveness toward me. Thank You for washing me clean through the blood of Jesus. Today

*I choose to forgive (name of the person) the same way You
forgave me. I let go of any offense, anger, and unforgiveness.
I pray that You would bless them, protect them, and that
they would feel Your goodness and love today! In Jesus's
name, amen.*

After you say that prayer, breath in and out. Allow the Holy
Spirit to fill your heart with His love, goodness, faithfulness, grace,
and mercy. Lastly, get rid of the paper
on which you wrote these names and
memories; do the physical act of
throwing away these hurtful wounds.

I had to do this multiple times over
the years, and paper by paper, memory
by memory, the Lord began to purify

**Forgiveness
is putting
the ball in
God's court.**

my heart, mind, and emotions. Forgiveness is putting the ball in
God's court.

RESPONDING WITH FORGIVENESS

Some of us struggle with forgiveness because we like things to be
fair. We want justice! My mom swore I was going to be a lawyer.
I love to fight for my rights and the rights of those I love. In the
beginning of our marriage, I hated that Martin would not speak up.
This man wouldn't even hurt a fly.

Once, there was an accusation
against him about being in a
relationship with a young lady at

**"When in doubt,
throw it out."**

the church (this was a couple years before we got married). Well,
that young lady was engaged to another guy. I know, big church
gossip! You know what Martin did? Nothing! What! Trust me, I
was mad, too! I wanted to go to the church and speak to the pastor

myself and tell them all it was a lie. Martin continued to serve God and attend the church. A couple months later, the truth came out, and he was innocent! It was all a made-up story.

I never understood why he didn't fight for himself. Well, now, years later, it is one of my favorite qualities that Martin holds. He only speaks up when it is wise to do so. I learned to love that about him once I realized the reward of staying quiet and letting God speak for us and fight for us. When we are hurt, struggling with unforgiveness and offense, we bleed and make it all much messier.

> *Do not take revenge, my dear friends, but leave room for God's wrath, for it is written: "It is mine to avenge; I will repay," says the Lord. On the contrary: "If your enemy is hungry, feed him; if he is thirsty, give him something to drink. In doing this, you will heap burning coals on his head." Do not be overcome by evil, but overcome evil with good* (Romans 12:19–21).

Here's what I've learned from a pastor: when emotions are high, wisdom is low. The times that I have spoken up, I was very emotional and I lacked wisdom. I just wanted to give in to my emotions and my prideful heart. My motives didn't allow me to think of the other person. My motive was to make things right. I wanted things fair! I wanted to win this battle! But what does God say? Do not take revenge. Leave room

When emotions are high, wisdom is low.

for God's wrath! Most of the time, defending ourselves is not wise, and we create more of a mess instead of solving the problem.

So how do we respond to criticism, offense, and hurtful actions from others?

To help you remember and make this practical, I am using the word "SOUL" as an acronym for Surrender, Out-Good Them, Understanding and Wisdom, and Lavish Yourself in His Love.

Why SOUL? To remind you that when we respond to hurt the way that the Lord wants us to respond, our souls are at peace, living in freedom and joy.

SURRENDER

We surrender it to the Lord. Matthew 11:28 says, "Come to me, all you who are weary and burdened, and I will give you rest." This verse is not only talking about being burdened from our everyday responsibilities—it's also talking about our emotions. Those things in our hearts that are burdening us, causing us to be weary. He wants us to rest in Him with our thoughts and emotions. Sometimes going out on a walk and breathing fresh air, allowing those emotions to settle, can help with bringing your nervous system to a state of relaxation. This will even help your physical body to experience rest in Him as you surrender it to the Lord.

OUT-GOOD THEM

> *But to you who are listening I say: Love your enemies, do good to those who hate you, bless those who curse you, pray for those who mistreat you. If someone slaps you on one cheek, turn to them the other also. If someone takes your coat, do not withhold your shirt from them. Give to everyone who asks you, and if anyone takes what belongs to you, do not demand it back. Do to others as you would have them do to you. If you love those who love you, what credit is that to you? Even sinners love those who love them. And*

if you do good to those who are good to you, what credit is that to you? Even sinners do that. And if you lend to those from whom you expect repayment, what credit is that to you? Even sinners lend to sinners, expecting to be repaid in full. But love your enemies, do good to them, and lend to them without expecting to get anything back. Then your reward will be great, and you will be children of the Most High, because he is kind to the ungrateful and wicked. Be merciful, just as your Father is merciful (Luke 6:27–36).

God understands that it is a sacrifice when we do good to those who have hurt us. But it is pleasing to Him. I know that sounds easier said than done. But can you imagine if everyone in the world would approach every problem with a posture of harmony and doing good to others, even those who have hurt us? That's when we would really experience peace in the church.

I remember the day when a coworker said some very hurtful things to me. Things I was not expecting to hear from someone who had said they loved me. She used very painful words that made me cry a lot. I sat there and just heard her bash every single

Doing good to others when they hurt us is forgiving them, extending a hand of grace and mercy.

ounce of confidence I had in myself. The Holy Spirit told me to stay quiet, and He gave me this immense peace that I had never felt when encountering trouble because my initial tendency is to defend myself. But I didn't that day. I sat there and listened to her. When she finished, I told her that I forgave her, and I even asked her for forgiveness. As I was leaving, the Holy Spirit told me to give her a card with Colossians 3:12–14 written on it and to give her flowers. Clearly, this is not something that would come naturally to me. But I obeyed. It was a sacrifice He asked me to make. A couple days later, I brought flowers and wrote that card for her. After that, the Lord did something so beautiful in our relationship He healed it and restored it. Doing good to others when they hurt us is forgiving them, extending a hand of grace and mercy. This is not to show off my actions. This is to show that when we are

> We can all agree that the Lord is always working. Whether we see the fruit of it yet or not, we know that the Lord always has a purpose and plans for our circumstances.

obedient to the Holy Spirit and allow Him to dictate our actions over our emotions, He can clean up our mess. He creates unity within the body of Christ.

UNDERSTANDING AND WISDOM

James 1:5:

> *"If any of you lacks wisdom, you should ask God, who gives generously to all without finding fault, and it will be given to you."*

We can all agree that the Lord is always working. Whether we see the fruit of it yet or not, we know that the Lord always has a purpose and plans for our circumstances. I

> His love is what defines us, not the criticism of others.

believe that when we're able to understand that the Lord has it all under control, we are able to experience an unconditional peace that only comes from Him. We do not need to know His ways in order to feel His peace. But we do need to understand that His ways are higher and better and whatever circumstance you are facing He is the one at work. Ask the Lord to give you wisdom on how to respond to the situation. Do you need to speak to the person about it? Do you need to leave it in God's hands and just pray for them? If speaking up is the wise thing to do, ask the Lord to guide you through every word and give you peace when it is the right time to speak up.

LAVISH YOURSELF IN HIS LOVE

1 John 3:1:

> *"How great is the love the Father has lavished on us, that we should be called children of God! And that is what we are!"*

After experiencing criticism, hurtful comments, and painful situations, we need to remember that we have a God who loves us more than anyone else in this universe. His love is what defines us, not the criticism of others. We are children of God! The way I've done this practically is by sitting in God's presence and allowing His love to embrace me and minister to me. Jesus was criticized, hated, and accused; yet, He still called Himself the Son of God knowing His identity in the Father. So, I encourage you to do the same. Remind yourself that you are loved, accepted, called, and chosen by the King of kings. That your identity as a child of God cannot be removed and that nothing can separate you from God's faithful love.

Forgiveness is not a one-and-done deal. It is a daily commitment to check our hearts and ensure that there's no unforgiveness unattended in our hearts. I still continue to practice some healthy soul habits to ensure my heart is aligned and righteous before our Father.

Here are two things that I continue to do daily:

First, pray for and bless those who have hurt and offended me.

This was the biggest game changer for me. Sometimes when I sit in God's presence in solitude, I either feel or remember the way someone made me feel. I now realize that this is the Lord's way of making me aware of something that I have ignored, but sitting in God's silence allows my heart to slow down and consider if my heart is righteous before Him.

> **Forgiveness is not a one-and-done deal.**

Second, examine what I can learn from specific situations.

Most of the time there is a conflict, misunderstanding, or uneasiness in my heart about something or someone that God is trying to make me aware of, something He wants me to grow in. Allow the Holy Spirit to bring self-awareness so that you are able to grow from every situation and get closer to God.

RECONCILIATION

It's been seven years since the Lord has healed the painful wounds of my church hurt, and even though I have forgiven all those individuals, there has still not been an opportunity for reconciliation with some of them, and that's okay.

I think some have the misconception that forgiveness means reconciliation, and some hold back from forgiving because they think they have to restore the relationship, but that's not entirely true for every relationship. We see plenty of examples in the Word of God of people who had conflict and forgave but did not reconcile for some time or ever.

Joseph and his brothers. Joseph was sold by his brothers; they betrayed him and hated him. Joseph forgave his brothers, but their relationship was not immediately reconciled; it took years for trust to be rebuilt (Genesis 45:1–15).

David and Saul. They experienced years of conflict. Saul felt jealous and insecure toward David. David had the opportunity to kill Saul plenty of times, but he did not, which showed that he in fact forgave Saul for the many times he tried to kill him. It was not wise for David to try to pursue a reconciliation with Saul. Unfortunately, Saul continued to pursue vengeance to kill David up until his death. David understood that forgiving him and allowing God to take over the situation was wiser than taking matters into his own hands (1 Samuel 24:26).

Jesus forgave Judas even before the famous kiss of betrayal. Jesus welcomed Judas to eat with Him and to follow Him, and He poured into him and loved him. But at the end, Judas's actions did not give the opportunity for reconciliation (Matthew 26:14–16; 26:47–50).

Forgiveness is something we do for ourselves. It is an act of surrendering our hurt and pride and letting God do His will over the situation. Forgiving is giving up the poison so that we can live. Reconciliation is a two-way street. It depends on the other person too, not just you.

> **Forgiving is giving up the poison so that we can live. Reconciliation is a two-way street. It depends on the other person too, not just you.**

I am confident Jesus would have liked to reconcile with Judas, like He did with Peter. Peter denied Jesus three times. I find it so interesting how Peter's denial is far more preached about than the reconciliation that took place between Jesus and Peter after His resurrection. Maybe because it is human nature to focus on things that are hurtful rather than the good that comes out of hurtful seasons.

After Jesus's resurrection, He appeared to Peter. Every time I read this passage I get so emotional, mainly because God used these specific verses to bring a lot of healing to my heart. In John 21:15, Jesus asks Peter, "Simon son of John, do you love me?" Guess how many times He asked him this same question? That's right, three times! The same number of times Peter denied Him. Jesus wasn't asking Peter if he loved Him to remind Himself of how much Peter loved Him. Even Peter told Him, "Lord, you know all things; you know that I love you." This question, and the answer to it, was for Peter! He wanted Peter to hear himself saying, "Yes, I love you," and to focus on that! This was Jesus's way of redeeming Peter's denial, and a reminder to Peter that Jesus knew that he loved Him. Not only did Jesus forgive him, but He then said to him, "Feed my lambs. . . . Take care of my sheep" (John 21:15–16). Jesus was showing Peter that He trusted him with the most precious thing to Him: His sheep! This was possible because even though Peter denied him, Peter stayed and was honest about the posture of his heart. He didn't leave or disappear. Peter regretted his actions, he decided to stay, and he repented and truly loved Jesus. And because of this, there was space for reconciliation.

Judas, oh poor Judas. My heart hurts for him, and I truly feel bad for him. I struggled a lot for some time knowing that he killed himself. I remember watching the movie *The Passion of the Christ* and thinking to myself, "No, don't kill yourself, Judas, Jesus is about to die for your sins! Jesus already forgave you!" Judas felt remorse and he hated that he sold innocent blood. He let guilt and shame overpower the love he had for Jesus. My heart hurts to write this because I think about the many people walking around feeling remorse, shame, guilt, and unforgiveness toward themselves, one another, and even to God. These emotions only lead to death. Spiritual death. They hold people captive to the plans of the enemy over their hearts, minds, and souls.

I encourage you to ask the Holy Spirit to give you discernment over any relationships that still need time to reconcile. Sometimes it is not wise to reconcile right away because that person may continue hurting you and end up creating more wounds of unforgiveness. So, friend, today, forgive those who have hurt you. Ask the Holy Spirit to let you see those who you still have to forgive. Leave the reconciliation to the Lord's timing. Those people that hurt you are also in their own process—we all are!

A couple years ago, the pastor that caused most of my church hurt connected with me and asked me for forgiveness. She listed the things that she recognized she had done wrong and acknowledged that she had hurt me, my husband, and many others. This happened years after I had forgiven her! I was in her shoes years ago myself. I reconnected with those I had unintentionally, or intentionally, hurt and offended. It's God's way of being in all of our stories of redemption. That His grace is extended to even those who have hurt us.

Those people that hurt you are also in their own process— we all are!

My friend, I understand that this may have been a challenging part for you to read, but I assure you that once you forgive and release the offense, you will experience healing and freedom. According to the Bible, forgiveness is not just about letting go of resentment; it is also about acknowledging that God has forgiven us and extending that same forgiveness to others. In Matthew 6:14-15, Jesus teaches, "For if you forgive other people when they sin against you, your heavenly Father will also forgive you. But if you do not forgive others their sins, your Father will not forgive your sins." God doesn't want you to remain enslaved to the past. Jesus has already paid the price for your wounds; now it's time for you to choose healing and freedom for yourself!

> **Forgiveness is not just about letting go of resentment; it is also about acknowledging that God has forgiven us and extending that same forgiveness to others.**

Dear heavenly Father,

Thank you for your forgiveness and gentle love as you expose those areas in my heart that are still hurt and wounded. I pray for Your love to continue to embrace me. Thank you for the healing you are already doing in my heart and soul. I pray that as I continue to read this book you continue to work in my heart. I pray that you remind me of any area of my heart that still needs to heal and forgive others. Have Your way Lord! I want Your perfect will upon my life. I want to grow closer to you as I continue to read this book. Thank you for what you are already doing in me. In Jesus's name, amen.

CHAPTER 3

JUST LIKE DADDY

M ateo, our oldest son, was in a reading class online when the teacher asked the students what they wanted to be when they grew up. The other children's responses included teacher, policeman, Spider-Man, firefighter, doctor, and vet, but we were eager to hear Mateo's response. When it was finally his turn, he responded, "I want to be a daddy, and I want to work at a church doing production!" That was the sweetest answer! Mateo didn't say that because it sounded cool, he answered that because that is what he sees his daddy doing for a living. Mateo's number one hero is his daddy. He wants to be like him now and when he grows up. He wants to follow in the footsteps of his daddy. I told Martin, "No pressure, dude, you can't mess up. That kid is watching your every step!"

His desire to work at a church might change in the future, we're not sure. But what struck me about his response was that he did not care what anyone else thought. His teacher's response was "Oh nice, yeah that's obtainable," and it didn't even faze him. Because Mateo's confidence in what he wants to be when he grows up is set. He enjoys watching daddy doing what he does so much that he wakes up at 5:00 a.m. every Sunday to make sure he goes with dad early to church. He enjoys being around him. All he wants is to be with his dad and to be like him.

Mateo only sees how much his daddy enjoys being a dad and how he loves what he does for work. It is worthy of admiration and respect. Mateo doesn't see the sacrifice of being a dad. He doesn't see the long nights Martin spends putting production projects together. He doesn't see the number of meetings his dad attends or the amount of learning he does to be where he is at. He doesn't know the stress his dad goes through on weekdays at work and on Sundays at church. He only knows that he wants to be like his daddy.

Mateo holds such a firm confidence in his daddy that nothing changes the way he feels about him. Nothing changes the way he loves, admires, respects, honors, and values the relationship he has with his dad.

Mateo's identity in who he is right now in his prime years of childhood is found in his daddy, in the relationship he has with him. He does not only see Martin as his father, but the important thing here is that Mateo sees himself as a son of Martin.

Martin could be the greatest father, but if Mateo doesn't identify as a son, what would it matter if he had a good dad? It is easy to see that when a child does not have a parent in the picture they are more prone to struggle with rejection, low self esteem, trust issues, emotional instability, attachment and abandonment issues. I don't think it is a coincidence that when we don't accept our identity as a child of God we as well struggle with these issues too.

We know that we have a good, good Father! We know that He is faithful, kind, merciful, graceful, and loving. We know that. But we still have not fully grasped the reality that we are His children.

How different would our walk with the Lord be if we saw God as our Father and if we saw ourselves as children of God?

Maybe you did not have a mom or dad growing up. If not, I am so sorry! Maybe that is why you have struggled with self-love, acceptance, and rejection. Or maybe you walked away from your children because you did not see yourself as being worthy of raising them and you've carried that guilt for years. I am so sorry! God wants you to know that you are His child and He has lavished His love on you! You are loved, forgiven, and accepted!

Or maybe you can relate to my story. I grew up with a mom and dad, but I struggled with self-worth. For some reason, the enemy was always after my identity. I was bullied, molested, and rejected as a child. I hid it from my parents because I did not want to get in trouble - another lie of the enemy. I found my worth in the honor roll ceremonies at school and in winning competitions; I found it in accomplishments and in my physical appearance. I didn't struggle with my confidence physically or academically. I knew I was pretty, smart, funny, and talented.

As an adult, I've found my worth in my abilities to get things done, in diplomas, in my career, in my marriage, and I have to admit that for a very long time, I found my worth in ministry and in the validation of my leaders.

There is no title or affirmation greater than the love that He has for me, simply because I am a child to my heavenly Father.

One of the toughest seasons in my walk with God has been finding out who I am as a child of God. Understanding that before I am a wife, a mom, a pastor, a friend, an author, a photographer, or an entrepreneur, I am a *child of God!* There is no title or affirmation greater than the love that He has for me, simply because I am a child to my heavenly Father.

A CHILD OF GOD

Somehow, the enemy is always after our identity as children of God. We see it all throughout Scripture. From Genesis, when Adam and Eve lost their rights as a son and daughter because the enemy tempted them by placing doubts about God in their hearts. Moses was filled with so much self-doubt, battling with God and questioning his worthiness and ability to fulfill his role. Jacob deceived his father to obtain Esau's birthright and later had an encounter with God and wrestled with Him all night. But at the end, God changed his name from Jacob to Israel, and he received a new identity. I can only think about the amount of times that the Lord spends wrestling with us because of our own stubbornness, when all He wants from us is to stand still, trust Him, and allow Him to love us.

Another example is when King Saul did not fulfill his calling because he wasn't focused on his assignment. Jealousy and comparison ended up ruining his life and his confidence as a king. Truth is, that the root of these character and identity issues is that these people did not see themselves as children of God.

In Matthew 4:1–11, Jesus Himself was tempted by Satan. But I don't believe the temptation was in the things he offered to Jesus. The temptation was in the first question he asked. The devil asked Him, "If you are the Son of God…" The devil was coming for his identity as a son. As a child of God. Before the enemy can tempt us with anything, he's always going to come for our identity as children of God. He knows that if he can

Before the enemy can tempt us with anything, he's always going to come for our identity as children of God.

take that away from your identity, he can take anything else. Truth is, anything that can be taken away from you was never really yours from the beginning. So titles like wife, pastor, lawyer, doctor, preacher, and teacher can be taken away from you. The only thing that belongs to us is our identity as a child of God. But it is up to us to receive or give that identity away. The devil knew that if Jesus gave His identity as the Son of God to the devil, he would fill His heart with doubt and fear. A heart full of doubt and fear is paralyzed from doing God's will. When we don't understand our identity as a

> **Truth is, anything that can be taken away from you was never really yours from the beginning.**

child of God, we become prideful. We think it's all on us, when it's not. Our faithful Father is a good Father who wants to fulfill every need in our lives and hearts. He wants to take that heavy yolk from our shoulders, and He wants to give us life, joy, love! But how can He do His job as a Father when we don't recognize that we are His children? How do we proclaim our identity as a child of God?

"Yet to all who did receive him, to those who believed in his name, he gave the right to become children of God—children born not of natural descent, nor of human decision or a husband's will, but born of God" (John 1:12–13). It is our choice to be His children and He is ready to give us that right! The only reason we wouldn't have that right is if we choose not to have it and decide to reject God's love and identity. "He was in the world, and though the world was made through him, the world did not recognize him" (John 1:10). The enemy takes that away from us and we have to claim it back! "He came to that which was his own, but his own did not receive him" (v. 11). The enemy makes us blind to our identity as God's children, and he will use anything and everything to make us not claim our right as children of God!

Make that choice today! Choose to be a child of God! Claim your identity! Simply accept it and recognize that He is your Father and you are His child!

For a long time I struggled with comparison, validation, and false humility.

> **The enemy makes us blind to our identity as God's children, and he will use anything and everything to make us not claim our right as children of God!**

COMPARISON

Comparison was stealing my joy of walking with Him. Comparison did not allow me to stay in my lane and focus on Jesus, and it did not allow me to enjoy what the Lord was doing in me and through me. Comparison stopped me from living in the present in the fullness of the Lord. I allowed comparison to bring many frustrations not only to my heart but also to the people around me. Comparison blinded me from seeing who God created me to be.

> **Comparison blinded me from seeing who God created me to be.**

Not long ago I had a bad scare while driving. My little one was in the back seat, and as any toddler that wants his mom's attention, he started screaming *mama*. I was trying so hard to give him my attention while keeping my eyes on the road. But at one point, I looked back to check on him, and out of nowhere I heard a car beeping at me. I was driving into his lane without knowing. I almost caused a car accident by not keeping my eyes on the road.

We can cause damage to ourselves and others by not keeping our eyes on our lane. By not paying attention to what God is asking us to focus on right now. By not keeping our eyes on our own race, and instead focusing on something or someone else that is not what God wants us to focus on. I learned that there are things that I am not called to or that are not in my capacity to do, and I need to be okay with that. I was too focused on the things I wanted to do but couldn't do. I was too focused on someone else's lane, and that caused a lot of frustration within me and put pressure on God's perfect timing.

The Word reminds us to "Keep your eyes on Jesus, who both began and finished this race we're in. Study how he did it. Because he never lost sight of where he was headed—that exhilarating finish in and with God" (Hebrews 12:2 MSG).

Keeping our eyes on Jesus means finding joy in the process. Comparison steals that joy! When we face trials and focus on comparing what life looks like for others, or what our lives used to look like, it takes away from what the Lord wants to do in our lives now. Fixing our eyes on Jesus means keeping it all about Him. And if we continue to compare ourselves to others, we are no longer keeping it about Him—we are bringing attention to ourselves. He wants to surpass our comparison and keep our eyes on Him because He finished the race and He is our ultimate example on how it's done.

> **Keeping our eyes on Jesus means finding joy in the process.**

VALIDATION

Seeking validation was not allowing me to enjoy the fullness of God's glory. I sought the validation of leaders instead of the validation that my heavenly Father had already given me. When we seek the validation of a leader, a pastor in the church, it can bring so much hurt to our heart and identity. We can't blame our leaders in the church for not affirming us when we're not sitting in God's affirmations over our lives. John 12:42–43 says that the rank leaders believed in Jesus but decided not to openly acknowledge their faith because they loved the approval and praise from men more than from God. Ouch!

Do we care more for the praise and approval of our leaders than for approval from God? I once did, but I was not aware of it until the day I stopped receiving the compliments and validation from my leaders. I began to think I was not doing enough, that I wasn't meeting their expectations, and that I wasn't doing a good job—just because I stopped hearing it from them.

> **Do we care more for the praise and approval of our leaders than for approval from God?**

I allowed the Lord to dig deep and search my heart. I recognized that I had not been doing this for Him for some time. Instead, I was doing it for the "Good job, Meri!" We have to understand that our reward is not here on earth. Our reward is in heaven! The Word says, "Blessed are you when people insult you, persecute you and falsely say all kinds of evil against you because of me. Rejoice and be glad, because great is your reward in heaven, for in the same way they persecuted the prophets who were before you" (Matthew 5:11–12). Wait a second! Jesus did not say blessed are those who their leaders recognize, affirm, and validate. That puts everything in perspective. Those who have been hurt, insulted, persecuted, and falsely accused because of Him are *blessed!* Seeking rewards because of what we do in the church will only lead to disappointments, unmet expectations, and hurt. Our reward is in heaven—not here! Seeking the validation of a human only causes us to drift away from the true love of God. The true love that wants to forgive us, affirm us, and embrace us with His grace and mercy.

Here was my problem: I wasn't resting in God's love,

Our reward is in heaven—not here!

so I felt the need to be admired by my leaders because of my accomplishments. There was so much freedom the moment I realized that I am already approved by God, and I have nothing to prove to people. My friend, do not settle for human love. Go after the Father; He wants you to return to that first love only found in Him!

FALSE HUMILITY

Walking around the church with the mask of false humility has hurt us and others. Not admitting and surrendering our pride is dangerous for our walk with God. For a long time I walked around with a posture of false humility. I don't think I understood the depth of finding myself in the Lord or knowing who I was in Him. We practice false humility when we intentionally devalue ourselves to appear humble, but being humble doesn't mean devaluing our accomplishments. False humility brings a lot of attention to ourselves, which takes the attention away from God. Did you realize that pride and false humility are both self-centeredness? I've learned that sometimes we take ourselves way too seriously.

One Sunday morning I was backstage getting ready to go onstage to give some announcements. I was so nervous about having a panic attack. I kept telling God, "Why do I feel so nervous? God, please take all this anxiety and panic away from me now." When out of nowhere, I felt His calming, loving, sweet voice say, "Why

We practice false humility when we intentionally devalue ourselves to appear humble, but being humble doesn't mean devaluing our accomplishments. False humility brings a lot of attention to ourselves, which takes the attention away from God.

are you making this about you?" Y'all! For real though! At that moment I realized that going onstage was not about me! Nothing I do is about me. It's about glorifying God and ministering the love of God, even if it's just through some announcements. So how do we let go of false humility? We remove ourselves from the moment and allow Him to lead the way. Allow His name to be glorified. Allow His name to be known, not yours. Ultimately, we gotta get out of the way!

I love Deuteronomy 30; what a reminder of the beautiful blessings found in our Father over our lives. He promises us that if our hearts stay obedient and follow Him with all our heart and soul, He will delight in us and He will make us most prosperous in all the work of our hands. He tells us to choose life, to choose loving the Lord our God, to listen to His voice, and to cling to Him. But in that same chapter it says, "But if your heart turns away and you are not obedient, and if you are drawn away to bow down to other gods and worship them, I declare to you this day that you will certainly be destroyed. You will not live long in the land you are crossing the Jordan to enter and possess" (Deuteronomy 30:17).

No, God is not a God who condemns us. But there are consequences when our hearts turn away from Him. Not because He wants to let us go, but because we create space for the enemy to come into our hearts and contaminate our minds, hearts, and souls. The Lord asks us to not bow down to any other god or worship them, and no, maybe we are not physically bowing

Anything that removes the Lord from being first place in your heart, soul, and mind takes His place as King of your life and is considered idolatry.

down to other gods or worshiping them like the Israelites did, but when we do start to put our leaders' validations before God, when we start to do things in our own strength, and when we stop praying to Him and seeking Him, we then start to remove the Lord from His position in our hearts, and we do fall into idolatry. Anything that removes the Lord from being first place in your heart, soul, and mind takes His place as King of your life and is considered idolatry.

In that same passage, the Lord tells us He will circumcise our hearts so that we may love Him with all of our hearts and souls, and we could live (Deuteronomy 30:6). All the character molding, the pruning, and the trials we go through, the Lord uses it to prune us so that our hearts become healthy. But it is our choice to either hold fast to the Lord in those seasons and persevere through the crushing or to allow pride to continue lingering around our hearts and not let circumcision take its full effect so that we can grow a healthy heart that beats for the Lord.

My friend, I encourage you to continue seeking Jesus! Jesus's confidence was in the Father, not in the applause of others or the recognition of the people. In order for us to be healthy spiritually, we have to stop comparing ourselves, stop looking for the validation of leaders, and stop walking in false humility. And we have to start sitting in His presence, start letting ourselves be loved by our good Father, start asking the Lord to prune our hearts, start removing ourselves from the equation, and start seeing ourselves how God sees us.

> **Jesus's confidence was in the Father, not in the applause of others or the recognition of the people.**

We have to start asking the Lord to remove our insecurities and give us more self-awareness of the areas He wants us to lay at His feet. We have to run to that first love and cling to Him every single day.

REMAIN

Jesus is our ultimate example of being confident in His identity as the Son of God. His identity in the Father was so firm that nothing could shake it. No devil, no Pharisee, no tribulation, no criticism, no question, no government, not even the cross! He never doubted His identity as the Son of God. Jesus knew and understood the value of being able to remain despite the suffering. That's why He tells us to remain in Him so that after He prunes us, trimming the areas that weren't pleasing to Him, He is now able to continue to work in us, but only if we remain in Him!

> *I am the vine; you are the branches. If you remain in me and I in you, you will bear much fruit; apart from me you can do nothing. If you do not remain in me, you are like a branch that is thrown away and withers; such branches are picked up, thrown into the fire and burned. If you remain in me and my words remain in you, ask whatever you wish, and it will be done for you. This is to my Father's glory, that you bear much fruit, showing yourselves to be my disciples. As the Father has loved me, so have I loved you. Now remain in my love. If you keep my commands, you will remain in my love, just as I have kept my Father's commands and remain in his love. I have told you this so that my joy may be in you and that your joy may be complete* (John 15:5–11).

Jesus knew and understood the value of being able to remain despite the suffering.

In the same way, a branch derives its life and vitality from the vine; so too do we draw our spiritual sustenance and identity from our relationship with our Heavenly Father. Remaining in Christ is more than a religious obligation; it is a profound expression of our identity as children of God. It is an acknowledgment of our utter dependence on Him for our very existence and a surrender to His will and His ways. You will only be able to bear fruit as a child of God when you remain in Him. Let me put it this way: you can't expect an orange to grow from an apple tree. You will bear fruit according to whatever you are attached to.

> **You can't expect an orange to grow from an apple tree.**

Remaining in the vine is where we find our true identity! That's when we begin to understand what it truly means to be His children. When what He is doing in us is far more important than what He is doing through us. When the fruit of what we do is a resemblance of His holy character and not our wicked ways. When we love the things He loves and hate the things He hates. When God is our only source of inspiration, motivation, and passion. When His presence is what we crave daily. Where nothing shakes our faith, and where our hearts finally reach the fullness of a good and loving Father.

> **Remaining in the vine is where we find our true identity!**

> **He is inviting you to remain in Him to receive your true identity as a child of God.**

Today, He is inviting you to remain in Him to receive your true identity as a child of God.

Remain in Love with God (Matthew 22:37).

In order for you to receive your identity as a child of God you need to remain in love with the Father. The same way a marriage takes work to stay in love is the same way God asks us to put in the work to continue to fall in love with Him every single day. Through prayer, reading His word, to live out a holy and righteous life serving Him and seeking Him in spirit and in truth so that He continues to work in us for His glory.

Remain Loving People (Matthew 22:39).

Jesus treated people with love, patience, kindness, gentleness, and for sure had a lot of self-control when others mistreated Him. I have learned from the hurt I've experienced in the church that those leaders or people who did not have their identity rooted in Christ were the ones who would mistreat others with hate, dishonor, lack of empathy, anger, greed, pride, lying, and gossip. Our identity as children of God is highlighted by the way we treat and love others.

Loving God and loving people were a crucial part of my journey toward healing, one that the Lord led me to explore deeply. In the pages ahead, I'll explain that process and share the valuable lessons that God used to bring healing into my life.

Remain Pure in Heart (Proverbs 4:23).

Guarding our hearts involves protecting this understanding of our identity in God. It means staying alert against influences that may lead us away from this truth or cause doubt about our worth and value in God's eyes. Just as the verse emphasizes the importance of guarding our hearts above all else, knowing our identity as God's children is foundational to how we navigate life's challenges and decisions. That is definitely easier to write or say than to do. There have been days this year where I've asked God to put a shield in my heart so that offense and hurt could not enter, just so that God would protect my heart from any hurt that might affect the way I see myself as a child of God.

Remain Accountable (2 Corinthians 13:5).

Having an identity rooted in Christ involves regularly examining ourselves to ensure that our beliefs, attitudes, and actions align with His teachings and example. We assess whether our thoughts, words, and deeds reflect the character of Christ and His love. The verse reminds us that as believers, Christ dwells within us through the Holy Spirit. Our identity in Christ is not merely an external label but a transformative reality. Understanding this truth shapes how we view ourselves and others. It empowers us to live in the awareness of Christ's presence within us, guiding, empowering, and transforming us into His likeness.

Remain in Your Calling (John 3:16).

Our identity in Christ forms the foundation of our existence, shaping how we perceive ourselves and the world around us. Rooted in the unconditional love and grace of Jesus, our identity transcends earthly labels and circumstances. When we understand our identity in Christ we are able to embrace our unique calling and purpose. Remaining in our calling requires steadfastly abiding in Christ, allowing His truth to permeate every aspect of our lives. It means aligning our thoughts, words,

Rooted in the unconditional love and grace of Jesus, our identity transcends earthly labels and circumstances.

and actions with His will, trusting in His guidance and provision. Just as branches derive their sustenance from the vine, we draw strength and vitality from our intimate connection with God. By remaining in our calling, we bear fruit that glorifies God and reflects His love to the world, fulfilling the divine purpose for which we were created.

In order to heal from the hurt you've experienced in the church it is vital that you know your identity in who your Father is. It's recognizing that you are deeply loved, cherished, and valued by the Creator of the universe. When you see yourself as a child of God, it transforms how you view yourself and others. You begin to walk with a new-found confidence, knowing that you are not defined by your wounds but by the unconditional love and grace of your Heavenly Father.

Dear heavenly Father,

Thank You for Your redemption, for Your forgiveness, for Your love. Thank You for being a good Father. Thank You for that privilege. I pray that in seasons or moments of doubt You would help me remember my identity in You! Help me remember that anything can be taken away from me except my right as Your child, unless I let the enemy take that right. I pray that You give me the strength, the grace, and the wisdom to always remember and own my right as Your child! Thank You for the reminder that this is not about me. This is about You! This is about bringing glory and honor to Your name. I ask that You forgive me for any time that I have made this about myself. I pray that You help me continue to seek You in spirit and in truth. I pray that You help me remain, to sit in Your presence and seek Your love, affirmation, and grace. I love You, Lord. In Jesus's name, amen.

When you see yourself
as a child of God,
it transforms how
you view yourself
and others. You
begin to walk with a
newfound confidence,
knowing that you are
not defined by your
wounds but by the
unconditional love
and grace of your
Heavenly Father.

CHAPTER 4

FALLING BACK IN LOVE

M artin and I were newlyweds, and we were broke (in every sense of the word—financially, spiritually, emotionally). I was in college finishing my bachelors, working full time at preschool, I had to be at church every single day, and I was learning how to be a wife. A lot of sudden changes all at once, to say the least.

Even though I was at church every single day and completely consumed by it, I had no genuine community; well, now I know that, but back then I thought I did since we were surrounded by so many people at church. I remember feeling lonely and misunderstood so many times. My pain was too deep, my hurt had created permanent scars, my emotional health was a roller coaster, and people that we deeply loved were leaving the church feeling hurt and so lost, the church was divided. My heart hurt so profoundly that I couldn't bear the abuse, and I wanted to fix the church myself, but I also thought, *How can I if I'm part of the problem?* So I gave up on church, I gave up on trying to be this perfect church leader, I decided to stop painting the perfect picture of my life—it was time to surrender!

I remember one day, I sat in my closet, just wanting to hide. I was feeling so much shame for the toxic leader I had become. I was exhausted, tired, overwhelmed, burnt out by my choices and the toxic leadership. I remember sitting there crying and asking God, "Lord, please let me see the things You hate and help me love the things You love." I don't even know where that prayer came from; I guess I was so tired of hurting others and allowing pain to control my relationship with the Lord. At that moment I just wanted my heart to draw closer to Him. This was the moment I realized that my motives, my thoughts, and my heart were so far away from God.

I had my Bible with me (by a miracle, because I never used to read it), but that day I needed to run to God and sit in silence with Him. I didn't need a whole three-hour church service, I didn't need a prophet, I didn't need a pastor, I didn't need the validation of the people around me, I didn't need a listening ear, I needed God Himself! I wanted His presence. I needed to let it out to my Father, the one I served every single day but had no communion with. I remember that day, sitting there in my tiny walk-in closet, crying out to Him, and when I opened the Bible, I kid you not, this was the verse that my Bible landed on:

> *Teacher, which is the greatest commandment in the Law?"*
> *Jesus replied: "Love the Lord your God with all your heart*
> *and with all your soul and with all your mind." This is*
> *the first and greatest commandment. And the second is like*
> *it: "Love your neighbor as yourself." All the Law and the*
> *Prophets hang on these two commandments* (Matthew 22:36–40).

I began to sob! I began to ask God for forgiveness! In that moment I felt His overwhelming love and conviction. I had not been loving God and His people. I had done the total opposite. I "loved" God when I went to church to perform. I say "perform" and not "serve" because I was not doing this with pure intentions, with the right heart—I was going to church to show off. To show off the strong leader that I was. I was broken and hurt, and I was just hurting others. To show off my talents and not give God the glory through them. To show off my outfits, to even show off my husband and how much we did. I thought we were irreplaceable. No one else was the power couple that we were. Oh boy, was I wrong! (I am laughing at myself as I write this, remembering how immature and prideful I was! Thank you, Jesus, for your redemption).

Through my years of healing, the Lord has walked me through different seasons to show me what it really looks like to love Him with all my heart, soul, and mind. In the next few pages we're going to dive into what the Lord has taught me about what that truly really means. I pray these words resonate with you and impact your heart to grow closer to Him, as they did for me.

LOVE GOD

LOVE GOD WITH ALL YOUR HEART.

In Luke 8, Jesus teaches the parable of the sower:

> *A farmer went out to sow his seed. As he was scattering the seed, some fell along the path; it was trampled on, and the birds ate it up. Some fell on rocky ground, and when it came up, the plants withered because they had no moisture. Other seeds fell among thorns, which grew up with it and*

*choked the plants. Still other seed fell on good soil. It came
up and yielded a crop, a hundred times more than was sown*
(Luke 8:5–8).

Jesus then explains the parable to His disciples:

*Those along the path are the ones who hear, and then the
devil comes and takes away the word from their hearts, so
that they may not believe and be saved. Those on the rocky
ground are the ones who receive the word with joy when they
hear it, but they have no root. They believe for a while, but
in the time of testing they fall away. The seed that fell among
thorns stands for those who hear, but as they go on their way
they are choked by life's worries, riches and pleasures, and
they do not mature. But the seed on good soil stands for those
with a noble and good heart, who hear the word, retain it,
and by persevering produce a crop* (Luke 8:12–15).

There's a very important concept to grasp in these verses: the
condition of the soil where the seed lands matters. The seed is
the Word of God, and the soil is our heart. Let me put it this way:
the condition of your heart is what truly determines how you are
loving God.

Remember King Saul and King David? They were both
anointed kings chosen by God. The Israelites respected and loved
the two kings because of their strong allegiance to God. But
what set David apart from Saul? His heart! Saul once was close to
God, but he did not guard his heart. Saul allowed pride, ambition,
disobedience, and jealousy to enter his heart.

These two kings were not perfect. They both sinned against
God. But the difference between Saul and David was that Saul
never repented and David did. The Word says that David was a
man after God's heart (Acts 13:22). David's heart was good soil.

The condition of your heart does not only affect you but those around you too. This makes sense as to why we see so much hurt in the church when the leadership does not have a healthy heart. The Lord commands us to guard our heart because everything flows from it. (Proverbs 4:23). We guard our heart because it is valuable. We care for, protect, and guard valuable things, right? I wouldn't leave my brand-new car unlocked, with the doors wide open, unattended in a dangerous neighborhood. Why? Because I know that I am putting my car in a dangerous area to get robbed. So why do we do that to our hearts? Why do we put ourselves in vulnerable situations or conversations that we know are only hurting ourselves even more?

Friend, I want to kindly remind you that the condition of your heart matters to God far beyond anything else. Let's be people of God who are good soil, that when we spend time with Him and read His Word, our hearts are fully ready to receive the fullness that He has for us.

LOVE GOD WITH ALL YOUR SOUL.

One of my favorite passages in Scripture is when Jesus is in the garden of Gethsemane right before He gets arrested:

Then Jesus went with his disciples to a place called Gethsemane, and he said to them, "Sit here while I go over there and pray." He took Peter and the two sons of Zebedee along with him, and he began to be sorrowful and troubled. Then he said to them, "My soul is overwhelmed with sorrow to the point of death. Stay here and keep watch with me." Going a little farther, he fell with his face to the ground and prayed, "My Father, if it is possible, may this cup be taken from me. Yet not as I will, but as you will" (Matthew 26:36–39).

This passage has ministered to me in so many different stages of my life. It has allowed me to learn more about the character of

Jesus in many different ways and has transformed my heart. The Word says that Jesus was feeling overwhelmed to the point of death! He was about to be betrayed and arrested. When I read this passage, my heart grows closer to Him and my love for Him grows deeper. It is a reminder of what Jesus went through to save you and me! It is a reminder of how Jesus was willing to go through the pain knowing what He was getting himself into. Some of us are scared to walk into new seasons because we are afraid of getting hurt or afraid of the unknown. Jesus was ALL in, y'all! He knew what was ahead, and He still did it!

This passage of Scripture does three things to my soul: First, it really puts into perspective some of my problems. Nothing I'm going through is equal to death itself. Second, it reminds me that when I am hurting, Jesus knows what that's like too. Third, my favorite thing is that it shows us what Jesus did when He was hurt-

> **Jesus was ALL in, y'all! He knew what was ahead, and He still did it!**

ing; He went away and sought the Father and asked for God's will to be done! He was honest with how He was feeling, but He did not walk away from what God was calling Him to do! Jesus gives us the perfect example here on what it looks like to love the Lord with all your soul. That even when we're hurting, overwhelmed, depressed, sad, or broken, we run to our heavenly Father. It's okay to tell Him how we feel! It's okay to let it out! That's what Jesus did!

A couple years ago, Martin and I experienced one of the most devastating times in our lives. We lost our brother-in-law and my father-in-law within a month. We were so broken! Nothing in that season made sense! Why would God take away our brother-in-law so young and full of life? Why would He leave my sister as a widow in her mid-twenties and alone to raise two babies? Why would God take my father-in-law and leave my mother-in-law alone?! Why would He take him away after losing my brother less than thirty days before?! I can't even list the number of questions I asked the Lord in that season. The amount of sorrow and hurt my soul was feeling was unbearable! In the midst of our brokenness, the Holy Spirit reminded me of the garden of Gethsemane. He showed me that there was no pain my soul was feeling that Jesus hadn't felt.

Every pain you've experienced within the church context or life in general, Jesus has felt it too. He already took the hit for us! He already suffered for you and me. When we are hurting, walking away seems like the best option, but is that the Father's will? Before you give in to your emotions and pain, run to the Father and ask Him for His perfect will. Not the will of your soul or emotions, His will. Like Jesus did! He said, "My Father, if it is possible, may this cup be taken from me. Yet not as I will, but as you will". What a powerful statement of true surrender. I believe the Word tells us to love the Lord with all of our soul because He wants ALL of it! The good, the bad, the raw, the honest truth! He wants our true emotions! Jesus was the only perfect man to walk this earth; in that moment He felt weak, tired, scared, and yet He ran to the Father. His soul was sold out for God's will! When we choose God's will over our pain, it doesn't deny the existence of our desires or pain, it simply says that we're not going to put anything before God. So how do we do that? How do we ensure we are loving God with all of our soul?

We do what Jesus did! "He fell with his face to the ground and prayed." He fell with His face to the ground as a sign of surrender

> **Every pain you've experienced within the church context or life in general, Jesus has felt it too.**

and humbleness! We surrender to the Lord, we leave our pride behind, and we recognize that His plans are greater than ours; we recognize that He will receive all the glory through this pain! That is what loving God with all of our soul means; that all the things we desire, all the plans, the thoughts, the emotions are all surrendered to His perfect plan. Why does it matter if we gain the whole world and forfeit our soul (Mark 8:36–37)? Why does it matter if all the things we want to accomplish in life come to pass, but our soul is lost?!

> **When we choose God's will over our pain, it doesn't deny the existence of our desires or pain, it simply says that we're not going to put anything before God.**

Jesus made the decision to first surrender and pray. It is so powerful when we run to the Father in prayer. When we surrender to the Lord, we empty ourselves. When we pray, we allow the Holy Spirit to fill us with His strength, courage, peace, goodness, and bravery to keep on going when our souls are overwhelmed! The Word says that Jesus repeated this three times, which reminds us that this is not a one-and-done thing. We continuously need to surrender our soul's desires and allow the Holy Spirit to fill us up.

LOVE GOD WITH ALL YOUR MIND.

When I was pregnant with our second boy, I was so set on giving birth unmedicated. So I asked all my friends who had previously done this about tips and tricks on how to give birth naturally. One of them recommended the book *Ina May's Guide to Childbirth* by Ina

May Gaskin[3]. This book not only changed my entire perspective on childbirth but also on the power of our mind. One of the most powerful things I learned is that giving birth is actually 80 percent mental and 20 percent physical. Say what?! You would think it is the opposite because of everything that a woman's body needs to go through. But nope, our mind is actually more powerful than our physical body.

In her book, she gives numerous examples and true stories about how the power of the mind is truly what matters when giving birth. Well, I can testify that this is true. The day I gave birth to our youngest boy was the most painful yet most magical day of my life. I was scared to give birth, mainly because the birth of our first child was traumatic. But I did everything in my power to make sure Martin and I were both prepared for that day.

As the contractions got super intense, I quoted Scripture; I reminded myself that I am strong, brave, courageous, and that my body was created to do this. I breathed in and out through every contraction. I did not tense up, I embraced the pain. In the moments I felt I could not bear the pain, my husband told me, "You are marvelous, you are strong, you have everything in you to give birth!"

I didn't do anything physical to make my pain go away. It was all in my thoughts and declarations. We did that for about three hours, and we fell asleep. I thought I was experiencing false labor since I was thirty-eight weeks pregnant. What I did not know then is that I was in full active labor, but because my mind was at peace and I was doing everything in my power to remain calm, my entire nervous system was ready to just rest. After four hours of sleep, I woke up and the pain was even more intense. That's when I knew it was show time! We had to go to the hospital.

---

[3]   Ina May, *Ina May's Guide to Childbirth* (New York, NY: Bantam, 2003).

The car ride to the hospital was no fun! I was so consumed with worry, despair, and anxiety, my mind forgot to stay calm. My contractions were unbearable and I could not walk! I was freaking out! When we got to triage, Martin held me and said, "Baby breath," and he helped me ground myself again. After the midwife checked on me, I was rushed to the labor and delivery unit. One of the nurses asked me, "Mom, would you like an epidural?" I said, "I think I can do it without it!" and she said, "You can do it!" When the nurse said that, I changed my mind from *I think* to *I can*! I began to tell my mind, I can do it, I am strong, I am brave. My husband continued to repeat the phrase "You are marvelous, you were created to give birth." Those words were everything my mind needed to hear to give me strength!

My husband, my mom, all those nurses and midwives were my support system. They were my biggest cheerleaders, and no one did anything physically to help me—they only reminded me how I was made for this and that I was doing a great job. You'll probably think I am lying if I told you that I did not feel some of the contractions. But it's true. My mind and my thoughts were firm on believing I am strong, I am brave, I am courageous, I was made to do this! In that moment I learned to confess what I wanted to believe, not necessarily what I was feeling. Loving the Lord with all our mind has a lot more to do with what we believe than what we feel! You possess what you confess!

About an hour or so later, the midwife said to me, "Mom, it is time to push!" I started freaking out again, and I felt every ounce of every contraction at that point! I felt weak and ready to give up. I asked for everyone to be quiet and to just play the worship music we had on in the background. I started to sing "Promises" by Maverick City Music, I again grounded myself, and I commanded my mind to remember the promises of the Lord over my life and the life of our baby boy. I sang an entire Maverick City Music song, and if you know them, you know those songs are eternal. But in that moment I was so focused on aligning my mind back to peace!

A few minutes after that, our baby boy was in my arms. I was able to do this not because I had exercised throughout my entire pregnancy or because I was fit and strong physically. I was only able to do it because of the grace of the Lord and the strength that my mind holds over my body! Every birth is different, and please don't feel ashamed or guilty or judged because you had a medicated birth or a C-section. Trust me, I know giving birth is not easy, and I am sure a lot of what happened in your birth story was actually outside of your control. Please find comfort in knowing that the birth story the Lord chose for your child was His plan and all for His glory. The point of sharing my story is to tell you that I have experienced firsthand the power of the mind and how things are possible if we put our heart and mind to it.

Loving the Lord with all of our mind also means staying in community with others to help us resist negative thoughts and to assist those positive thoughts. That, my friend, is why we need to stay in the church, connected to other believers who are willing to step in the gap for us, even when we're weak. If you noticed in my birth story, I was not alone. I had an amazing support system, one that helped me stay strong when I was weak. When I couldn't even believe it for myself, they encouraged me and had faith for me. When I was no longer mentally strong, they were there to refill my mind with strength and courage. During the COVID pandemic in 2020, we saw an increase in mental health issues arise, with isolation being identified as the primary cause. The only moment in scripture we see the enemy tempt Jesus was when He was alone in the wilderness. I believe this is highlighted in the scriptures to show us the danger of isolating ourselves. The enemy uses isolation to hinder the wonders God wants to do in our lives. If you have isolated yourself because of the hurt you've experienced in the church I want to encourage you to run back to community and allow this community to speak life into your thoughts.

How to Strengthen Your Love for God:

Okay, this is all great, but how do we really get to a place where our hearts are pure, our souls are aligned to God's will, and our minds and thoughts are captive to God's perfect will over our lives? I have some practical steps for you that I continue to practice and have been a huge part of my healing journey.

1. **Renew Your Heart, Soul, and Mind through Prayer**

Romans 12:2 (ESV) says, "Do not be conformed to this world, but be transformed by the renewal of your mind, that by testing you may discern what is the will of God, what is good and acceptable and perfect."

The enemy wants you to isolate yourself when you are weak; the enemy wants you to leave the church when they hurt you; the enemy wants you to walk away from God when He doesn't "answer" your prayers. But we need to renew our minds, the motives of our hearts need to align to His, our soul and emotions need to be reminded that we are here for His will not ours. What does that mean? It means to set our hearts and minds on things that are above, not on things that are on earth (Colossians

> **But we need to renew our minds, the motives of our hearts need to align to His, our soul and emotions need to be reminded that we are here for His will not ours.**

3:2). It means to lay down the ways of this world and the negative thoughts we have about ourselves, others, and God. I encourage you to journal those negative thoughts that aren't true, noble, right, pure, lovely, and admirable (Philippians 4:8). You've got to get it out of your system and surrender it at the feet of Jesus. The way we know our thoughts are from the Lord and are aligned to His good and perfect will is when our thoughts produce life and peace. Are your thoughts producing life and peace over you and the situation you are facing?

For those who live according to the flesh set their minds on the things of the flesh, but those who live according to the Spirit set their minds on the things of the Spirit. For to set the mind on the flesh is death, but to set the mind on the Spirit is life and peace. For the mind that is set on the flesh is hostile to God, for it does not submit to God's law; indeed, it cannot (Romans 8:5–7 ESV).

During prayer, ask the Lord to give you a mind and heart that is set on the things of the Spirit, thoughts that are praiseworthy and honorable to the Lord. Through prayer, take those thoughts and statements and make them obedient to the Lord (2 Corinthians 10:5).

Pray for God's protection for your heart, emotions, and mind. Ask the Lord to protect your heart from offense and hurt. Let me tell you, it works. I've experienced it firsthand! When I feel the anxiety wanting to overtake my heart in that very moment I declared John 14:27: "Peace I leave with you; my peace I give you. I do not give to you as the world gives. Do not let your hearts be troubled and do not be afraid." Through prayer is how I give the Lord all my worries and anxiety. I give Him space and permission to work in my heart to protect it and guide it so that when offense, anxiety, and hurt comes my heart and mind are protected and at peace.

2. Recite Scripture

In order for us to love God with all of our heart, soul, and mind we need to be connected to His very own Word. God's word will protect our hearts and minds from our own sinful ways. We can't live a fulfilled life without filling our hearts and minds with God's word.

> *"How can a young person stay on the path of purity? By living according to your word. I seek you with all my heart; do not let me stray from your commands. I have hidden your word in my heart that I might not sin against you."* (Psalms 119:9-11)

I believe there is a powerful reason why God told Joshua to keep the book of the law always on his lips and to meditate on it day and night (Joshua 1:8), because truthfully, reading the Scriptures is what helped ground his mind on things above. It helped him keep his eyes on the big picture, reminding him of the promise that God had for him and the Israelites. The Lord told Joshua to be strong and courageous four times in that same short passage, and not because who he was against was bigger than the God he served, but because he needed to remind himself of who made him strong and courageous. He also told him not to be afraid, mainly because fear begins in the mind and then penetrates the heart if not dealt with. The Word of God is true and tangible, and before we preach it to anyone else, we have to preach it to ourselves.

Jesus was the perfect example—I mean, He always is, right? He quoted Scripture when the enemy tempted Him in the wilderness (Matthew 4:1–11). The devil was getting in Jesus's mind, tempting Him with everything he could. But how did Jesus fight him? With the Word of God! And He did not only do it once in that passage,

He declared the Word of God as many times as He needed to to fight this battle against the enemy.

My friend, if there are lies of the enemy that you are believing, I encourage you to declare the Word of the Lord over your heart, mind, emotions, and identity. Renewing the mind is replacing those lies with His Word! Guard your thoughts and heart with God's word. Our thoughts can easily spiral into negativity, fear, or doubt if left unchecked. Replace negative thoughts with God's promises and truth. "Take captive every thought to make it obedient to Christ" (2 Corinthians 10:5).

Lies	Scripture
I am not enough.	Psalms 139:14
I am not called.	Isaiah 43:1
I am not worthy.	Matthew 6:26
I am not anointed.	Psalms 23:5
I am not accepted.	John 1:12
I am not loved.	Ephesians 3:19

3. **Remain Present**

A key aspect I have learned about loving God with all my heart, soul, and mind is to slow down and be present. Breakfast and dinner times are extremely important and special at the Duarte household. Every day, we sit at the table and enjoy our delicious breakfast cooked by Daddy, and dinner is usually cooked by Mommy. At the table as a family, we pray, hear our boys' silly stories, answer random questions they have about life, and during dinner we talk about our favorite moments of the day and anything that happened that made us feel sad or upset. No phones are allowed at the dinner table, the TV is off, and we are fully present in the moment. It's been a ritual of ours as a family, and as much as I love and truly appreciate this family time, I can't lie: many times I've sat at that table thinking about the billion things I had going on.

At the breakfast table I think about my super long to-do list, all the meetings that are ahead of me. At the dinner table I think about the many things I did not accomplish and all the meetings that went wrong or weren't productive. My mind runs at a thousand miles per hour. I can't even tell you how many times I've sat in our prayer room ready to spend time with the Lord and the same thing happens: I start thinking of what I need to do next and how I gotta hurry up because we can't be late to work and the school car line.

There's been so many times that I've caught my mind being somewhere else and not where my feet are at. For a couple years now, I've been practicing and reminding myself, "Meri, be where your feet are at." I constantly have to ground myself in the moment. My heart and soul can be at peace with where I am, but where is my mind? Our mind needs to be aligned with our heart and soul so that our entire being is whole in one place. Truth is, your heart can be in it but not your mind, and He wants us whole and fully present in whatever it is that we are doing. Our mind is a battlefield and we need to align our mind with the heart of the Father. If the enemy can't tempt you, he will keep you busy. The enemy wants our minds rushing, thinking about the next thing. If we fully enjoy and live in the present, we are able to see God's blessings through a different lens. We're able to fix our minds and hearts on the things that truly matter and approach life from a place of gratitude and joy.

About two years ago, I asked the Lord to help me in this area of my life because sometimes I think I am superwoman and that doing five things at the same time is the best way to do things. Well, it's not. I was mad at myself for allowing those thoughts to steal the joy of being present in the moment with my family. I remember one morning when I was so exhausted and I felt the Holy Spirit telling me to rest in Him, to worship Him. I put on my husband's worship playlist—he's a musician, you know he has the best playlists—and I just broke in His presence. Practicing a regular time of praise and worship in the morning has helped me align my mind, heart, and emotions to be fully present in His presence. You see, when your heart, soul, and spirit are giving Him all the glory and honor, your mind has no other option but to be fully present in His presence. Your mind is reminded that nothing else matters but His presence! What He has to say! What He has done! Being fully present with the Lord allows the Holy Spirit to dig in those deep spaces of our mind, soul, and heart and gives Him space to renew us and sanctify us.

4. **Remember God's Armor**

> *Put on the full armor of God, so that you can take your stand against the devil's schemes. For our struggle is not against flesh and blood, but against the rulers, against the authorities, against the powers of this dark world and against the spiritual forces of evil in the heavenly realms. Therefore put on the full armor of God, so that when the day of evil comes, you may be able to stand your ground, and after you have done everything, to stand.* (Ephesians 6:11-13)

In order to love God as He wants us to, we need to guard and protect our hearts, souls, and minds against the schemes of the enemy. Spiritually clothing ourselves with the armor of God is something we can't forsake. It's as simple as reading Ephesians 6:10-20 every morning before starting your day and declaring it over yourself. In order to confront spiritual challenges, we must equip ourselves with spiritual tools.

- The belt of truth: God's unwavering truth, His Scripture. While His truth remains constant, it is constantly being revealed to us. Therefore, seek to understand God's truth revealed in Scripture and integrate it into your life accordingly.
- The breastplate of righteousness: Jesus's righteousness is the only way for us to be righteous. We have to remember that Jesus alone makes us worthy of God's unending love.
- The shoes of peace: Jesus said that He was leaving us with a gift—peace of mind and heart. Putting on the shoes of peace means that we do not only have it but that we bring His peace everywhere we go. We are His peacemakers.
- The shield of faith: Trusting in God's ways and character helps to extinguish the attacks of the enemy. The attacks like anxiety, fear, or depression. It is our faith that helps us stand firm and protects us from letting those attacks come in between our relationship with God.
- The helmet of salvation: Our minds are an active battlefield. It is important to declare the truth over our thoughts of our Salvation comes through Christ alone, and nothing can separate us from Him.
- The sword of the Spirit: Scripture clearly describes this "sword" as the Word of God. Everything else in the armor is used to protect us, but with the sword we are able to fight back with God's truth. We must be in the word of God to ensure we know how to use it when those spiritual attacks come.

We may not have control over the situations that come our way, but we do have the power and authority in Christ to stand firm and remain pure in heart, mind, and soul.

LOVE PEOPLE

But it doesn't end there! Remember the verse said to love the Lord with all your heart, soul, and mind. So what comes next? "Love your neighbor as yourself" (Matthew 22:39).

All of the sudden loving God seems pretty easy compared to loving our neighbor. Am I right? Or am I the only one?

We may not have control over the situations that come our way, but we do have the power and authority in Christ to stand firm and remain pure in heart, mind, and soul.

Oh my goodness, I can barely love myself is what I thought when I read this verse for the first time. How could I possibly extend love to someone else when I can barely extend grace to myself? Well, after years of reading this passage and studying it deeply, I've come to the conclusion that I cannot love my neighbor without loving myself first, because how you treat others exhibits how you really love yourself. But not the type of love that the world describes as self love. Self love is selfish. It seeks the benefit of one. At one point I thought I had finally hit a season in my life where I was loving myself, but the way I was treating others did not exhibit that. Because at that point, that was my ego loving myself. The world's definition of loving yourself first is idolatry to oneself. But that's not how God defines loving ourselves. Loving ourselves means seeing ourselves how God sees us. He sees us as His children—His most precious creation. Here is what I've learned about loving myself: I accept myself through the eyes of God; I receive God's love, I receive God's forgiveness, and I let God define me. Because once I accept the way He loves me, defines me, forgives me, and accepts me, then I can do the same for others through God's lens, not my own.

> **Loving ourselves means seeing ourselves how God sees us.**

You know who knows how to love people well? I think you know the answer by now: Jesus!

In John 15:12-17 He said to us:

> *Love each other as I have loved you. Greater love has no one than this: to lay down one's life for one's friends. You are my friends if you do what I command. I no longer call you servants, because a servant does not know his master's business. Instead, I have called you friends, for everything that I learned from my Father I have made known to you. You did not choose me, but I chose you and appointed you so that you might go and bear fruit—fruit that will last—and so that whatever you ask in my name the Father will give you. This is my command: Love each other.*

It is impossible to remain in the vine without loving one another. It is impossible to remain in the vine without forgiving one another, without serving one another, without believing in one another. And it's impossible to please God without loving one another.

Jesus came to teach us how to love one another.

Jesus . . .

- believed in people
- had compassion for the broken
- fed the hungry
- set the captive free
- healed the sick
- forgave without keeping a record of wrongs
- befriended people even though He knew they would betray Him
- loved unconditionally

Jesus loved Judas unconditionally. Did you realize that Jesus knew Judas was going to betray Him? And He still let him sit with Him, He still washed his feet, He still poured into him, and even believed in him! You know what's even wilder? When Judas gave Jesus up to the soldiers and gave Him a kiss on the cheek, Jesus's response wasn't "Oh, you betrayed me!" Instead, Jesus replied, "Do what you came for, friend" (Mathew 26:50). Jesus called him *friend*! That is what the Lord means by loving your neighbor! That regardless of what they are going to do to you or did to you, you still love them! Ah! I don't know if that hit you like a ton of bricks, but it hit me! Even when they betray you, speak falsely of you, hurt you, you still love them! Through loving people is the only way that we're able to see if we are really following Jesus's example.

> It is impossible to remain in the vine without loving one another.

Loving ourselves first means: loving others as you would like to be loved. See others as you want to be seen, speak to others as you would like to be spoken to, and treat others as you would like to be treated. We have to be completely consumed by the love of the Lord so that we are carriers of God's love and grace for others. I can testify for myself how much I have grown in the area of extending grace to others, but I would have never known that if I had walked away from the church. How could my character be put to test in isolation? We need to stay in the church so we can allow others to help us prune and grow in those areas of our lives. The Word says that "iron sharpens iron, so one person sharpens another" (Proverbs 27:17).

When people rub us the wrong way, it's not a red flag or some sort of sign to leave the church. It is actually a huge sign that there is something inside of you the Lord wants to refine.

I prayed the craziest prayer at the beginning of 2023. I asked the Lord for more wisdom and humbleness. Ha! The Lord had some deep pruning to do in my heart, and the instrument He used was people in the church to help me realize those areas in my heart that were filled with pride and foolishness. As much as we may want the church to be perfect, it will never be. Why? Because the church is filled with imperfect people like you and me. Like my pastor says, "Ministry is messy." Humanity is not perfect, and we live in a broken world filled with sin, hurt, evil, and hate. The church though is not just a building with four walls. The Church is you and me—the people of God. When we realize that *we* are the church and that *we* are the ones causing the pain within each other, wow, things change. This perspective of church hurt changes things because now we are coming from a place of asking what *we* can do to make sure this place is heaven on earth. Loving people well is to be Christlike! To be compassionate, patient, and loving like Jesus was when He was here on earth. The church exists so we can help people find salvation through Jesus, be transformed by the Holy Spirit (sanctification), help people find their God-given purpose, and make a difference.

> **The church exists so we can help people find salvation through Jesus, be transformed by the Holy Spirit (sanctification), help people find their God-given purpose, and make a difference.**

It was God's plan all along that He would send His Son to redeem His Church. ("Church," with a capital C, means "you, me, us," and "church," with a lowercase c, means "where we gather to worship Him.") He sent His son to give us the ultimate example of loving one another.

Redemption for the body of Christ looks like this:

> *Therefore, as God's chosen people, holy and dearly loved, clothe yourselves with compassion, kindness, humility, gentleness and patience. Bear with each other and forgive one another if any of you has a grievance against someone. Forgive as the Lord forgave you. And over all these virtues put on love, which binds them all together in perfect unity. Let the peace of Christ rule in your hearts, since as members of one body you were called to peace. And be thankful. Let the message of Christ dwell among you richly as you teach and admonish one another with all wisdom through psalms, hymns, and songs from the Spirit, singing to God with gratitude in your*

The church will never
be perfect because
it will always be
filled with imperfect
people. But the
church will always
be loved by God—no
matter how imperfect
it might look or how
broken it may be.

hearts. And whatever you do, whether in word or deed, do it all in the name of the Lord Jesus, giving thanks to God the Father through him (Colossians 3:12–17).

I love how the apostle Paul tells us to clothe ourselves. I believe the reason he tells us to clothe ourselves is because it's something that we have to do every single day. Every single day we have to choose to continue this ongoing journey of building His church with love, compassion, kindness, humility, gentleness, patience, forgiveness, unity,

> **My dear friend, let me remind you that whatever the enemy meant for evil, God will turn it into good.**

peace, and gratefulness. As we build His church with whatever kind of service that we do, let it all be in the name of the Lord Jesus, giving thanks to God the Father because it is only through Him — His sacrifice — that we are able and blessed to do this.

My dear friend, let me remind you that whatever the enemy meant for evil, God will turn it into good. The enemy might have used the brokenness of people in the church to hurt you, but God will redeem all that pain, suffering, and offense and heal you, comfort you, and love you.

The church will never be perfect because it will always be filled with imperfect people. But the church will always be loved by God—no matter how imperfect it might look or how broken it may be. Jesus already took that brokenness to the cross. Jesus already has died and resurrected for you, me, and all those who might have hurt us.

Dear heavenly Father,

I pray that You continue to help me and give me the strength to remain in You even when people hurt me. Help me remember every single day that the greatest command is to love you Lord and to love others! Lord, help me see your people how You see them. Lord, help me love them how You love them. I ask that you open the door and the right opportunity to have a conversation with people to resolve the issues and find forgiveness. Show me the areas you want to sharpen in me through others. Help me run to you and community when my heart, soul, and mind are weak. Protect my heart and mind from any schemes of the enemy. Lord, I thank You for healing me as I continue to grow closer to you. In Jesus's name, amen.

CHAPTER 5

THE TRIAGE ROOM

That day when I was in my closet crying out to God was pivotal for my walk with the Lord. I can't even recall how long I stayed in that tiny walk-in closet just crying out to God, asking Him for forgiveness and to fill my heart with His love, joy, peace, forbearance, kindness, goodness, faithfulness, gentleness, and self-control. I repented for all the hurt I had caused all these years, and I asked God to show me more of Him and to change my heart. Well, let me tell you, God heard that prayer! I felt His forgiveness, and He renewed so much in my heart that day. I fell in love with Him once again; I felt refreshed! Even though I had that beautiful encounter with the Lord, I still dragged myself to go back and serve at the church where we had been experiencing all this pain for the last eight years. It was hard because even though God started to show me all the things that were not His will over the church, He still did not give us "permission" to move to another church. I was a bit of a mess, I wanted to leave.

Martin prayed and also felt it was not the time for us to transition to another church. I was hoping Martin felt something different than I did, but that wasn't the case. So we stayed for another year, we remained obedient, and we decided to wait.

That year we saw and experienced even more hurt, pain, and abuse in the church. It did not make sense to us why God wanted us to wait another year. Truthfully, I wanted to grab my things and go. Years later I learned that the reason God had us wait another year to transition was because the place He had destined for us had not yet launched as a church. We often think, What if we would have moved and not remained obedient? Where would we be? God was preparing our hearts, our future home, our future pastors, and our healing place! All in due time, it would make sense.

IN THE WAITING

I learned a couple things about this season of waiting. I learned to serve the Lord unconditionally. I sought His kingdom first so that He would add everything else to our lives. I learned to serve the Lord with a limp! Even though I was going through a tough time in the waiting season, the Lord still used us and our pain to help walk with others. I learned to seek Him in spirit and in truth; I began a real relationship with the Lord. He wanted all my attention! He did not want me to focus on human leadership but godly leadership. I learned to treat people better and to genuinely love them, to have compassion over them, and to see them for who God created them to be. I learned how to be a better leader, treating others with kindness and respect, and I helped a few others create healthy boundaries. I learned how to be a submissive wife and how to be a good wife to Martin, one that prayed for him, followed his lead, and trusted him with the decisions for our marriage.

In the waiting, sanctification in my leadership began to happen. This process took years, but the waiting definitely exposed a lot of what needed to heal within me. As we waited, Martin and I became more aware of what toxic leadership looks like, and the Lord healed us from it. He gave us discernment not to fall into those patterns again and to genuinely lead people with the love of Jesus.

While we waited for God's direction for our next steps, He was doing some special work in our lives: Martin and I launched a small business (wedding photography and videography), I graduated from the University of Central Florida with a bachelor's in psychology and early childhood education, and I switched careers from teaching to working with children with special needs. We began the process of buying our first home, and ultimately, God gave us the biggest blessing: we got pregnant with our first child. So much was changing for us! God was clearly opening new doors for us, doors we did not even expect! All of this happened in just one year!

The beauty about waiting is that the Lord begins to answer other prayers that we don't even know we need answered. He begins to work in other areas of our lives unexpectedly. He sure knows how to surprise us! Our sacrificial obedience in waiting touches our Father's heart. I love how sometimes God can work and turn things around really quickly, but other times we have to wait, and embrace both seasons because we know that He is at work.

> **The beauty about waiting is that the Lord begins to answer other prayers that we don't even know we need answered.**

In seasons of waiting, I love to ground myself in Romans 8:28: "And we know that in all things God works for the good of those who love him, who have been called according to his purpose." What a beautiful reminder that the Lord is working in all things, always! He is working in the bad times, the disappointments, when we get that No, in the loneliness, in the hurt. He is working in our hearts, in the miracle, on getting us that Yes! Simply because He loves us! We have a purpose in Him, so even when nothing makes sense, when the waiting seems too long, when there's nowhere to go, when we can't hear His voice, He is using that for His purpose and glory. He is also using that for you, to build you, to mold you, and to strengthen your faith and perseverance.

TRANSITION

I remember the day I gave birth to our first son. I was forty weeks pregnant, I was about three centimeters dilated, and I had the worst contractions. The transition from being pregnant to meeting our baby boy was about to happen. But before we actually met our baby boy, some things needed to happen. I had all the boxes checked to go to the hospital. I don't know why I thought that as soon as I got to the hospital and told the nurses I was having contractions, they would immediately admit me, and I'd have this baby. Well, no, there was a process. The process of the triage room—the transition. I was so desperate to just get this baby boy out! I was ready for the reward of meeting my child. But there wasn't a room or a bed or a doctor or a nurse ready for me to be admitted to give birth. Waiting in that room was torture with all the pain I was in! I remember how my husband held my hand, looked straight into my eyes, and walked me through the breathing exercises. He put worship music on, he prayed for me, and at one point he had to fight for me. It seemed like no one cared that I was in so much pain and needed some help, so he stood in the gap for me. I was desperate to just

Being still is obedience, letting go of control, recognizing that it is not because of our strengths, talents, or knowledge that we are making it through, but because we start to understand the fullness and character of our Lord.

hear my name being called to move into a room and give birth. All I had to do was sit there, breathe in and out, try to stay calm, wait, and be still.

I wonder how many seasons of our lives we've been in the triage room, in the waiting, in a transition that feels more like torture than anything else. Where we feel like we're ready for the next chapter, the next move, the next step, but God is telling us "Wait, I have not opened any new doors yet!" These are the seasons when He asks us to be still. "Be still, and know that I am God; I will be exalted among the nations, I will be exalted in the earth" (Psalms 46:10). What's interesting is that Psalm 46 doesn't start or end with the phrase "be still." This psalm begins with mentioning the greatness of our Lord, One we can find refuge and strength in during moments of trouble. One who has all the power and authority even when the world is falling apart. He is our fortress! Being still is recognizing that we don't have the power to move on to the next thing until He says it's time.

Obedience was a huge part of our transition. I have learned that obedience looks very different in a season of transition. Transition is not about the end result—it's about what happens while we are in the process. The obedience that takes place during a season of transition happens in our hearts before God moves us. In this specific season of our lives we knew that the transition had already happened in our hearts, but the Lord was just preparing everything else for us to be on His timing, not ours. Martin and I did not want to "church hop." We did not want to move somewhere unknown and continue to get hurt. Ultimately, we did not want to be outside of God's will, and we

Transition is not about the end result— it's about what happens while we are in the process.

needed to remain obedient and continue waiting. God was continuing to move in our lives. At this point we had been married for three years, our first child was born, we bought our first home, but the question, *Hey, God, when are you going to give us the green light to transition from this church?* still remained in our hearts and prayers. It seemed like God had answered every other prayer except that one. But we knew we were walking in obedience, and the Lord would bless our obedience in due time. Even though we were still there, we knew we had to wait for our next step.

Being still is obedience, letting go of control, recognizing that it is not because of our strengths, talents, or knowledge that we are making it through, but because we start to understand the fullness and character of our Lord. Being still means allowing Him to fight our battles, giving Him space to do His work for us and in us, truly surrendering to the work of His hands. The moment I stood still, the moment I stopped fighting, the moment I stood quiet and surrendered, I realized the many seasons of my life that I had not let the Lord have His way. In seasons of transition when I was too busy trying to figure it out on my own, not learning from my own mistakes, not understanding that He wanted to do more for me and through me. The moment I let Him be God over my life, be the ruler of my decisions, be the love of my life is when I understood what true surrender meant.

You see, sometimes we think the transition is the hard part, and that can be because it requires us to be still, to let go of control and let Him be God. It requires a lot of faith, obedience, and patience. But if we look at the transition season as one that brings us closer to our Father, one that

Because the blessing that is in the process is far more beautiful than the sacrifice we had to endure.

builds our faith, one that changes our hearts, we would do it all over again! You know why? Because the blessing that is in the process is far more beautiful than the sacrifice we had to endure.

The best thing I can compare this to is parenthood. Having the first child is hard! Ask any parent. But for some reason, most of us choose to have a second child. And if you are a second child, you're a blessing, and your parents love you a lot. I promise. But, wow, if we had the first child and it was hard, why did we decide to have a second child?

I'll tell you why. Because even though being pregnant, giving birth, and raising a child is hard, there is nothing more precious than the gift of raising a child. Let me put it this way: yes, going through that painful season then was hard, and going through this painful season now is hard, but we would do it all over again because of the fruit that comes out of it.

The fruit in which we grow closer to our heavenly Father, the fruit into which we mature spiritually, and the fruit where our Lord gets exalted and glorified through the trial.

Friend, I encourage you to not lose hope when you are going through painful transitions. Hold on to that promise the Lord has made over your life. He is for you, and He will never leave you alone or forsake you. There is a blessing in the process, I promise!

WAITING IS TO SURRENDER

I have learned that even though waiting seasons really hurt and stretch us in different ways, something beautiful comes out of them for the glory of God. Waiting is to surrender. Surrendering our own desires, surrendering our own agenda, and surrendering our own timing. Something powerful happens when we surrender to the Lord. He begins to mold us. We give Him space to work within us. We allow Him to have His way in us, and there is nothing more pleasing to the Lord than a heart that is willing to be molded in His timing and in His way. It is in the waiting where we get molded and shaped into the child of God that He called us and created us to be.

Recently, I have found a love for things made out of clay. Not long ago, I bought this beautiful vase made from clay at HomeGoods. I love it because it has some intentional imperfections and uniqueness to it. I also love it because I bought it as the final product—I did not have to go through the process of making it. Agh! Sometimes we want that. Sometimes we want God to just do the thing and present the final product to us. We don't want to go through the process. Everything finished is beautiful,

> **It is in the waiting where we get molded and shaped into the child of God that He called us and created us to be.**

but there's actually more beauty in the process because we learn so much about God and ourselves.

I have learned a thing or two about making a jar of clay. Before the clay has any shape or value to it, it has to go through the throwing, trimming, glazing, and reduction with fire. Friend, all the hurt, the pain, the molding, the crushing has not been in vain. There is so much value, power, and anointment being poured out to you as you get molded, so don't give up. I promise you that the Lord will make something beautiful out of this painful season. The apostle Paul says we have treasure in jars of clay. But those treasures can only be found in the throwing, trimming, crushing, and persecution (2 Corinthians 4:7). Even though this season is painful, the Lord promises us we will not be destroyed!

Our sufferings display God's power! God is more evident in our lives in those seasons of waiting. If you and I are anything alike, then we both love to know what's next. I am a planner. I need things on a schedule. Well, that's not exactly how God works. He is a planner, and He has His ways set before us. But if He showed us what was next, what He has in store for us, we would never be able to grow our faith and maturity in Him. In this season of waiting know

> **Our sufferings display God's power! God is more evident in our lives in those seasons of waiting.**

that He will have His way and will be glorified through your story.

Friend, I encourage you today to not focus on your afflictions or pain but to reflect on God's promises. What are the things He has promised over your life? One of them I know for a fact is that He has promised a purpose and a calling over your life. Sometimes we want to rush the process, but nothing rushed is ever done well. If the potter rushed to finish the creation of his clay, he would eventually destroy the clay. I can't even tell you the number of things I have rushed through in life and later regretted because I realized that I did not learn the lesson entirely. There is a time for everything: a time to mourn, a time to cry, a time to wait, a time to move in faith, a time to be molded, and a time to see the fruit of the process in the waiting.

You see, removing the suffering and the pain in the process is not the solution.

We need to surrender to the potter's hands. Our hearts need to surrender to the Father's will. Making the jar is not truly about the end result; it is all about what the potter does in the molding! There is beauty in the messy process. There is growth in the process.

The potter builds and shapes our characters, hearts, desires in the process!

Maybe you are waiting for a big miracle. A positive pregnancy test result, a son or daughter to come back home. Maybe you are waiting for a spouse, the opportunity of a lifetime, a new home church, or for God to speak into the next season of your walk with Him. Or maybe you find yourself reading this book because you are currently in a season of waiting and healing from the hurt that the church has caused you. Waiting is not easy, but I encourage you, my friend, to stay in the process.

During the process, our hearts need to remain moldable. Clay remains moldable by adding water to it. Reading and studying the Word of God is the water our hearts need to allow Him to soften our hearts and mold us according to His perfect will.

God is a gentleman, and He will never force our hearts to be molded if our hearts are hardened. He wants a heart of flesh, not a heart of stone (Ezekiel 36:26). Our heart needs to be submerged in prayer, in the Word of God, for it not to harden.

The hardest part about learning how to mold clay on the potter's wheel is learning how to center the clay. If the clay is not centered on that wheel, it will be nearly impossible to create something out of the trimming and shaping. In our walk with the Lord it can be hard to remain centered in Him, but Paul reminds us, "Therefore we do not lose heart" (2 Corinthians 4:16–18). Don't lose love, passion, hope, faith, zeal in the One who is molding you with His own hands. "Though outwardly we are wasting away, yet inwardly we are being renewed day by day. For our light and momentary troubles are achieving for us an eternal glory that far outweighs them all. So we fix our eyes not on what is seen, but on what is unseen, since what is seen is temporary, but what is unseen is eternal."

When we are going through the crushing, we fix our eyes on Him, we forgive, we examine ourselves, and we ask God to let that mold us. Right now the waiting and the molding may seem like a waste of time but not inwardly. He is doing something so special, unique, and beautiful inside of you. He is at work, always!

So, friend, you need to remain centered in the potter's wheel. Being centered in the potter's wheel means you still show up! You still pray, you still worship Him, you still read His Word, you still serve Him! You let nothing shake your faith and who you are in Him! Being centered in Him means fixing our eyes on Him on the eternal because the pressing, the crushing, the shaping is temporary. Jesus had to remain centered when He felt the crushing weight of the sin of this world. He said, "Father, forgive them, for they know not what they do." (Luke 23:34 ESV) He centered His heart, His pain, and His attention on forgiveness.

When we are going through the crushing, we fix our eyes on Him, we forgive, we examine ourselves, and we ask God to let that mold us. Right now the waiting and the molding may seem like a waste of time but not inwardly. He is doing something so special, unique, and beautiful inside of you. He is at work, always!

The apostle Paul describes us as a "lump of clay" for a special purpose (Romans 9:21). Why a lump? Because without the clay, there is no vase for Him to make. If there is no vase, then how can we pour unto others? You are His vessel! You are His jar! One He wants to use for a special purpose. The only way this lump of clay was able to have a special purpose is because it remained surrendered and centered in the potter's wheel and hands.

WELCOME HOME!

After a few weeks of prayer and fasting, we felt like the Lord was giving us a small opening to transition out of the church we had been attending for the last ten years. I asked Martin if he was okay if I visited a church near our new house. He gave me the go-ahead—I was so excited! I remember walking in and immediately loving it. But I don't know if I would say I loved the church—I just loved the idea of moving on and settling right there. I was willing to settle because I was desperate to move on, and I did not want to be still anymore. Can you blame me? I had been dying for something new for the last three years. I was in a season of so much confusion, I had no community, the world felt lonely, and I was crying all the time. I couldn't breastfeed and that caused so much mom guilt. I had lost so much weight, I didn't want to eat. I was dragging myself to do things that I usually loved doing before. I had no one to talk to about motherhood and what I was going through, mainly because I had closed myself off. I had built some brick walls that only God would tear down in due time.

My heart breaks just writing about that Meri. Martin was also feeling so broken; he never voiced it, but I knew. We were both zombies, which naturally happens when you are a parent to a newborn, but I am referring to our hearts and spiritual walk. We were so dead, longing to be alive. So dead, longing for something new, something colorful. We didn't know exactly what we needed or wanted, we just knew it wasn't what we had been living for twelve years.

I went home excited to tell Martin about the church. I hyped it up so much that he actually went with me the following Sunday. I was sooo excited, I felt like it was the first day of school. Well, we get to the church, we walk in, and immediately Martin says, "This is not it." I turned and said, "What? You haven't even seen the service." He said, "We'll stay for the service, but, baby, this is not where God wants us." I wanted to throw the biggest fit. How? How could God not want us here? How could God bring us here to a church super close to our house, and this not be it? But, in that moment, I remembered to be a submissive wife and to listen to my husband, the head of our home, and trust that the Lord would show him our next step. Goodness, that was hard! But I knew I needed to trust the Lord and that He was guiding my husband.

That week I was very sad, and I felt somewhat spiritually homeless. At this point, we both knew God was giving us the green light, but to go where? I am not naturally the most patient person, so this unknown next step was very frustrating. I soon learned that the Lord just wanted me to lean in and continue to submit to His plans. In unknown seasons there are a lot of emotions that come in waves. Sometimes we feel patient and encouraged that God's got it, and other times we're frustrated and want answers now! And that is okay! We are human beings with real emotions. The Lord wants us to surrender to Him and plant ourselves in His grace and love. So that's what I did. That week I prayed and fasted. It had been about two years of waiting, and I could no longer bear the pain. Two years may seem like nothing for you, maybe you have been waiting for an open door or for God's next step for longer than that. I understand your pain too; I understand your despair, but hang in there, my friend. God's got this! Maybe we can't relate to the Israelites walking around a desert for forty years, but we can relate to the desperate "What now, God? You took us out of Egypt and now we're just wandering around! Great!" No kidding, I was waiting for God to reveal something to Martin like He had revealed to Moses. Ugh, I know I was being such a brat! But because I was a brat, the Lord continued to mold me and teach me that it was all in His time. He was not done with me. He was pruning so many areas of my heart. One of them was trusting His timing. You see, God's perception of time is not our perception of time. I needed to trust that His ways will always be higher than mine, that His plans will always be better and greater than mine. So I needed to continue waiting.

For us, this season felt as if we were in the operation room, and the surgery would be successfully done soon. We were on our way to the recovery room to embrace our journey of healing and wholeness.

A week later we traveled to Miami to shoot a wedding, and we decided to stay the entire weekend to visit family and friends. On Sunday my best friend invited us to her church. As soon as we stepped into VOUS Church, we immediately loved it! We left that place feeling encouraged, motivated, and with so much hope that soon we would find our church. I believe God gives us moments to remind us that He has not forgotten about us or our prayers. Moments to remind us to hope again, reminders that He is not done and that He is with us in this season of staying still in the midst of the unknown.

On our drive back home, my best friend's sister randomly sent us a message telling us about a former professor at Southeastern University who recently opened a church in Orlando, Florida. She sent us the church's Instagram handle. We jumped on to the church's podcast, and within four hours of our drive we had listened to several episodes. We cried in every single one of the messages. The Lord was clearly speaking to us; He began answering so many questions we've had and filled us with a love for the church again. We knew we needed to visit Journey Church.

Finally, Sunday came! Once again, it felt like the first day of school, and I was so excited to check out Journey Church. As soon as we arrived, we felt so much joy. The parking people seemed really happy, and they were smiling at us. As soon as we started walking inside, we saw all of these beautiful smiles, and people we didn't even know asked if they could give us a hug. I remember one specific greeter walking in with us and offering us coffee and a donut. That's when Martin knew this was home for us.

I was shocked to see so many people genuinely happy to be there and happy to see us there. Before walking into the service, I noticed diversity in race and age groups. I also noticed the church was portable; I did not know what that meant for the church, but I was eager to find out and amazed that a high school would allow a church to be there every Sunday. I had never seen anything like that before, but for some reason I loved the way it made me feel.

We walked into the service and sat in the front row. We wanted the full experience. Worship started and I just broke into tears; I felt the Holy Spirit say, "This is a safe place." Ah, my heart still feels what I felt in that moment: each palpitation pumped feelings of peace, joy, and security. I felt as if the walls of my heart were finally starting to tear down.

When the preaching began, for some reason my guards went up again. What if the message is not biblical and the pastor starts asking for money? My heart and mind were still somewhat guarded from what I had experienced for the last ten years. But as soon as the pastor went onstage, I noticed how humbled and joyful he was to preach. He introduced himself: "Hello, my name is JJ, and alongside my wife, Liz, we have the privilege and honor of leading Journey Church as its lead pastors." Hearing the words "privilege and honor" allowed my heart to feel peace and safety again. It showed me that their hearts were pure, their motives to open, and this church was simply about loving God and people.

The pastor was excited, refreshed, and full of joy to be preaching. I needed to see that. I needed to see that the lead pastor of this church was passionate and that he actually loved and had fun doing what God called him to do. I wanted that too, not just in church but also in life, in motherhood. Truth is, my church hurt, pain, bitterness, and unforgiveness was leaking into other areas of my life. The message that day was titled Day Dreams, and it was everything we needed to hear in that season. It was all about allowing ourselves to dream again. I had forgotten what it was like to dream. We were at a place where every ounce of our energy, passion, and dreams had been in dry soil for years, and we were exhausted, drained, and burnt out.

But we have a God who loves us and redeems our dreams, and who is intentional in every season of our lives and wants the best for us. A God who doesn't think like us, who doesn't work like us. Even though I didn't know what His special assignment looked like for me, I did know that He loved me, that His thoughts and promises over my life were true, and that He would complete the good work He had once begun in my life. And that day He used that message to ignite in us a passion for the church again!

At the end of the service, we felt so full. We went back to the lobby and met the pastor. Martin held my hand, approached Pastor JJ, and said, "Hello, we are Meri and Martin, and we would love to make Journey Church our home!" I wanted to hug Martin right then and tell him I was so proud of him! I still tear up thinking and writing about this moment. This moment was probably a normal event for the pastor but not for us. We were broken; we carried so much unforgiveness, trauma, hurt, and painful memories. Hearing my husband say "this is home" felt as if we had been homeless for twelve years, and we had now finally found our safe place to flourish into what the Lord had called us to do. The pastor smiled so big, hugged Martin and me, and said, "Welcome home!"

That moment was everything I had been praying for and more. I realized that one of the biggest lessons the Lord wanted to teach us as a married couple during this season was our roles within the marriage. I wouldn't consider our marriage being at a broken place then, but I do believe our roles were dysfunctional, and we never realized it until that exact moment. We didn't realize that we did not have a good example in the church of what a godly marriage looked like, so we were on this path of trying to understand and live out what that looked like according to God's Word.

Martin was on his own journey to understand his position as the husband, priest, and leader of our home. I was learning how to be a submissive wife, understanding how to trust my husband, and letting him make godly moves for us. Watching my husband step into the fullness of the husband God was calling him to be and knowing I had stepped into allowing myself to be led, was something I had been praying for. This was such a core characteristic in our marriage that needed to be molded, and that day I saw the fruit of being a wife under the submission of a godly husband. I understood that a lot of the frustrations in our marriage in the past had come from my own hurt. I understood that allowing my husband to lead us encouraged him to step out of his comfort zone. I stopped trying to solve issues for us and decided to take them to the Lord in prayer again. I learned to be a wife with gracious words. I realized that when I wasn't trying to tell my husband what to do, he had the clear mind to listen to the Lord and lead our family into the perfect will of the Lord. God was pruning our marriage, and arriving at a new church wasn't only healing to our spiritual walk, but to our marriage as well. He was healing our hearts, and He started with our marriage.

Journey Church was our new home! It made me feel safe, loved, cozy, accepted, and warm. Home, where I am accepted with all my baggage and not judged for it. Home, where people love me because of who I am, not because of what I have to offer to the organization. Home, where I can be myself and put my guards down. Journey Church, our new home, a refreshing place filled with new dreams, new hopes, new beginnings, and new people.

Walking into Journey Church was just the beginning of my healing journey.

Dear heavenly Father,

I feel like an Israelite walking around the desert, not understanding this season or what You are doing. But I surrender today! I ask for You to intervene in this season of my life. I ask that You provide direction, wisdom, and guidance. I let down my guard and allow You to mold me and teach me Your ways. This transition is hard! Being still is hard! Waiting is hard! But I thank You for the process. I thank You for the lessons I am learning and the ones I have learned as I remain still in You. I ask You to give me the strength to continue to remain surrendered, trusting that You are my fortress and my good Father. I pray You open the right doors at the right time. I pray that You fill my heart with Your peace, knowing that Your timing is better than mine. I ask that You open the right doors for me and my family in this season. I trust You, Father! I trust Your ways, and I trust Your plans. In Jesus's name, amen.

CHAPTER 6
TAKE TIME

We met with Pastor JJ two short weeks after our first visit at Journey Church. He wanted to know our story. Oh boy! I don't know if he was quite ready to hear this broken girl. He just sat there and listened, and that impacted me. He actually cared to hear our story and genuinely wanted to get to know us. His listening ears made me feel acknowledged. Of course, I was so hurt that all I could talk about were the differences between our previous church and Journey Church.

I vividly recall the moment in the conversation when Pastor JJ said to me, "I am so sorry you have been hurt by the church!" Up to that point in my life, I had not been aware that I was hurt by the church. The whole time I was masking my hurt with anger, comparison, frustration, and bitterness. I teared up a bit; it was like he had diagnosed the disease with all the symptoms I had been experiencing for years.

Martin picked up on the conversation and said, "We want to get plugged in and start serving!" Pastor JJ's reply is something I think about often and the impact that it has in my heart until this day. He said, "As much as I would love for you two to start serving, please take time to rest and receive." Martin's response to that was, "That actually makes me want to serve even more!" We wanted to be part of a community in which we felt loved and accepted for the gifts God blessed us with, not because the church needed us. We were tired of feeling needed. We wanted to feel genuinely loved, wanted, and accepted.

I have learned that many people walk into church feeling like that. They want to feel loved and seen. Sadly, sometimes that's the opposite of what we do as church leaders. We focus on the experience aspect and forget the people. Don't get me wrong, the experience is important, but the people are God's priority. Sometimes people will not even remember what you said to them, but they will remember how you made them feel. People who walk into the church don't have to be hurt by the church to feel like that. Life has its own struggles and people may already feel broken. We, the church, the leaders, the people that serve, are responsible for making those people in the church feel wanted, seen, accepted, and loved. Jesus teaches us that.

In Matthew 11:19, "The Son of Man came eating and drinking, and they say, 'Here is a glutton and a drunkard, a friend of tax collectors and sinners.' But wisdom is proved right by her deeds." Jesus was described as a friend of tax collectors and

> **Sometimes people will not even remember what you said to them, but they will remember how you made them feel.**

sinners. Jesus gave us the ultimate example of ministry. He wanted to love and accept those who the experts of the Law pushed away, those who weren't worthy of God's love. But if you think about it, that's all of us. I am not worthy of God's sovereignty, love, and forgiveness. I'm not! But that is called *grace*, and that is what Jesus came to give when He walked this earth.

I remember the way I felt while talking to Pastor JJ because he saw my pain and acknowledged it, and he even called me out when I kept comparing Journey Church with our prior church. He said to me, "Meri, I understand you are hurt, but that pastor did the best he could." In that moment I knew that, yes, I was hurt, angry, and bitter, but I had also caused so much pain myself that I needed to give those church leaders and pastors the same grace that is given to me every single day.

> **No season is ever wasted if we go through those struggles with a teachable spirit.**

Martin immediately started serving at Journey. His process of healing was a bit different than mine. Even though we were both so hurt, his type of personality needs to connect to a community to heal. He naturally tends to isolate when he is hurting, so connecting with a community and serving were very important for him to heal. In my case, I tend to lean on other people when I am hurt, but if I am bitter I tend to bleed on others. No season is ever wasted if we go through those struggles with a teachable spirit. God wanted me all to Himself. He wanted me to depend on Him fully. This season of solitude taught me how to fix my eyes on Him, to seek Him when my heart felt lonely, and to bleed at the feet of the cross, not on other people. Eventually God took me into a season of community. Where I was able to lean on others in a way that allowed me to continue the healing He started in solitude.

SEASON OF SOLITUDE

There's so much power in seasons of solitude, and I believe there are specific seasons for it. In this specific season of my walk to healing, the Lord wanted me to go out of my way to seek solitude with Him. Solitude is different from isolation. Isolation is considered the evil twin of solitude. Why the evil twin? Because even though they might look the same, they are different: one works for your own good and the other works against you.

Isolation is what the enemy uses to deposit seeds of depression, loneliness, and anxiety. From the beginning of days, the Lord said it was not good for men to be alone. We were never meant to be in isolation. We need people on our side who will walk in the dark seasons with us. People who are willing to lift us up when we are down, who can minister the love of Jesus to us, and who will help us grow.

Isolation is what the enemy uses to deposit seeds of depression, loneliness, and anxiety.

Solitude, on the other hand, is a healthy habit. Jesus always practiced solitude. Every day He went away and spent time with the Father. Here are some examples:

Luke 4:42: "At daybreak, Jesus went out to a solitary place."

Jesus practiced solitude in the morning.

Luke 6:12–13: "One of those days Jesus went out to a mountainside to pray, and spent the night praying to God. When the morning came, he called his disciples to him and chose twelve of them, who were designated as apostles."

So before Jesus chose the twelve disciples, He withdrew! He prayed in solitude before making a decision.

Matthew 14:13: "When Jesus heard what had happened, He withdrew by boat privately to a solitary place."

After hearing really bad news, He prayed in solitude.

In Mark 14, Jesus did not go alone to the garden of Gethsemane. He took Peter, James, and John. He needed that community to be there with Him. Jesus knew what was about to happen. But even in that moment, He still withdrew to be with the Father.

Luke 5:16: "But Jesus often withdrew to lonely places and prayed."

I love how it says "often." It was not a one-time thing. It was not only when everything was going great or when He ministered and healed hundreds of people. It was not only when He was in His worst pain. It was often—meaning every day! No matter what type of day He had, Jesus went to spend time with the Father in solitude. We can't expect to hear God's voice when the voices of this world are louder than His.

If Jesus Himself needed time to get away from the hustle and bustle of life, what does that tell us about our own need to create that same space in our lives? I get the responsibilities, school, work, our families, even tiredness. But Jesus also had a job, Jesus also felt tired, Jesus also felt overwhelmed. Jesus, the man that loved people with all His heart, wanted and needed to be alone with His Father.

He needed to recharge! Jesus, even in His quiet time, was tempted by the enemy, so what makes us think that the enemy won't try to stop us or tempt us to not spend time with the Lord? The world out there is loud! So loud, it is hard to hear the Lord. There's so much going on! Our human brains can't take it and

> **We can't expect to hear God's voice when the voices of this world are louder than His.**

we need to withdraw, not only physically but also mentally and spiritually to be able to heal, hear God's voice, and recharge.

Solitude creates space for healing. I wasn't always great at sitting in silence at the feet of Jesus! It was hard. The seasons in which I've really lacked my quiet time, I noticed how much of a mess I can be; in all the ways emotionally and spiritually, I lack discipline, compassion, and grace for myself. Sitting in solitude with the Lord means sitting in our emotions, our grief, our hurt, our pain. Sitting in solitude with the Lord makes space for gratitude in our hearts. When we're on the go, go, go, we forget to stop, look around, and notice the detailed blessings the Lord has given us. When we're on the go, go, go, we don't schedule time to process these emotions; therefore, your emotions get a hold of you at unscheduled moments.

I've spent countless times in solitude, and not only has solitude helped me prepare for a long day ahead, but it has also helped me heal from past hurt and pain. I specifically remember a time when I asked the Lord to show me areas I needed to grow in. Even though I had prayed this prayer several times, I had not made space for Him to speak to me. The Lord can speak to us anytime, anywhere, through anything. But when we make it a priority to sit in His presence and allow Him to speak to us, He honors that even more and allows our humanity to surrender to Him to speak to us. If you have a doctor's appointment, you schedule it; if you have a date, you schedule it. If you have something important to do, you schedule it. So why do we overcomplicate scheduling time in solitude with our heavenly Father? The most powerful way the Lord has spoken to me has been in moments of solitude in His presence, and those have been the most evident and clear moments where He has pruned me, humbled me, and loved me.

The Lord tells us to come to Him, all of us who are weary and burdened, and He will give us rest (Matthew 11:28). So why don't we? We are all walking around carrying burdens from our childhood, from our jobs, guilt and shame, when all He wants is for us to come to Him and lay our burdens at His feet.

Time in solitude has set me free from the church hurt, the offenses in my heart, my parents' divorce, the unquenching pain of grief, and it continues to set me free every single day! Truth is, I cannot pour out to others if I'm not being poured into. I cannot be the servant the Lord wants me to be if I am far from hearing His voice. Spending quiet time with Him has allowed me to be in tune with His voice. It shuts off the noise and the anxiety of the world, it allows me to hear the Lord in ways I have not before, it helps me to make better decisions throughout my day, and ultimately and most importantly, it allows space for the Lord to do some serious work in my heart.

Truth is, I cannot pour out to others if I'm not being poured into.

Solitude sets us free; it heals us and gives us the strength to keep going. It is in solitude where He takes away our worries and burdens, and that's where we truly find heavenly rest!

Here are some practical ways you can practice solitude:

Wake up thirty minutes earlier, go into a space with minimal distractions, leave your phone behind, and get some water or coffee to help you stay awake. Grab a piece of paper and name it *"Brain Dump"*. In this brain dump, write down everything in your mind that's stealing your peace. Things that are holding you back from resting your mind and thoughts in Him. All the to-do lists, the worries, the thoughts . . . Let them out of your system.

Welcome Him into this space and moment.

Grab a journal, and as you sit in silence, allow the Holy Spirit to speak to you, and then write down whatever you feel or hear within.

I generally practice this for about ten minutes, and I can feel the love and peace of God embracing me. Sometimes I feel areas of my heart that the Lord wants me to surrender, other times I hear or see a verse that the Lord wants me to read, and I open my Bible and can tell that it was indeed the Holy Spirit speaking to me. After each moment of solitude, I play worship music and worship the Lord for a few minutes, pray, and read the Word.

LEANING ON COMMUNITY

"Not giving up meeting together, as some are in the habit of doing, but encouraging one another" (Hebrews 10:25).

During that time of practicing solitude with the Lord, I did not run away from the church; instead, I leaned on community. I was still intentional about connecting with others. You see, church is fifty-fifty! We cannot expect to feel welcomed when we are already coming in with walls up that we're not willing to tear down little by little. Going to church is just like any other relationship: you open your heart to the willingness of building a connection with others and allow others to pour into you.

Jesus practiced solitude as much as He connected with and poured into others. Jesus understood the power of community, connection, and relationships. The Lord

Jesus practiced solitude as much as He connected with and poured into others. Jesus understood the power of community, connection, and relationships.

wants to use community to heal you! The power of connection is one of the healing tools that helped me overcome the hurt, pain, and offense I had in my heart. Connecting with others made me realize that not everyone is out to get me and hurt me, but I never would have learned that if I had not given church another try.

A pivotal point in my healing journey was the day I joined a small group. After a few months of just going to church to receive the Word and sit in the services, I knew it was time to find some community. I felt safe, and maybe not 100 percent healed, but I felt like some wounds were starting to close up. I was ready to make some new friends. What I did not know was that this would be the start of getting to know my new church family.

I knew the Lord was asking me to lean in on the community I could potentially experience at Journey Church. But there was a bit of a personal issue. Sometimes I felt like I did not fit in—not because of the wonderful people at Journey, but because of my own hurt. I was afraid that I might hurt others, and I thought that Journey didn't need a toxic member. On some Sundays I thought that they had it all figured out and they didn't need me. On other Sundays I thought I had nothing good enough to offer. Of course, these are all lies from the enemy that he wants us to believe. It was the same hurt that only allowed me to think about myself and not about the body of Christ. Serving others is selfless, but my heart was not ready to give, or that's what I thought. So I joined a small group.

Joining a small group felt easier for me. I wouldn't be committing to too much, and I wouldn't have to share much of myself—that's what silly me thought. I was also being super specific on the type of small group I wanted to join. I wanted a small group with only women, but preferably women who weren't moms. Why not moms? Well, I was going through a rough time as a stay-at-home mom, I was just starting to heal from postpartum depression, and I did not want to open up. I wasn't ready to let people in. I also did not want to hear other moms complaining about their kids. I wanted to get out of the house and find a different type of atmosphere. I was clearly desperate for a genuine community.

Well, there was a small group that met my requirements, and I later realized this group was more than what I wanted—it was what I needed. The group was called Freedom. It was fifteen minutes away from our house and on Wednesday nights. It was perfect! In reality, I picked this group because it was convenient for me, not necessarily because I knew what Freedom small group was about. I did not know that the Lord was preparing every step of my healing and every chapter of this book specifically.

On Wednesday nights, Martin would get home from work, I'd hand him the baby, tell him dinner was served, give him a kiss, and out the door I'd go. I was desperate for community. I still remember my first day at the small group—I was so nervous yet excited to meet new people. I received my Freedom book; mind you, this whole time I still had no idea what the group was about. I'm actually glad I didn't know because I'm not sure I would have joined knowing where my heart was at that moment.

As soon as I got my book, I opened it and saw that the first page said, "And you will know the truth, and the truth will set you free" (John 8:32).

Oh boy! Did I just sign up to a group where I am going to have to open up and let all my dirty laundry out to strangers? In one second I thought about all the ways to get out of it, but I couldn't! Something in me knew that I needed this group more than anything.

We started the group by watching a video and while it was playing all I could think was *"this is a small group on deliverance!"*

All right, let me backup and explain why it was a shocker for me that I actually ended up in this group. Years earlier when I was a leader at the church my husband and I had attended for ten years, the leadership was taught how to perform deliverances with no biblical knowledge of why people "needed" deliverance. When someone was struggling with something, we were told that the solution was "they need deliverance" or "they are possessed by (you name the spirit)." There was no guidance, no biblical explanation, or any counseling they could go to and dig deep to actually give the people practical everyday resources that would help them understand the source of their spiritual issue and lead them to healing.

This specific issue had caused *a lot* of hurt in me and in other people at the church for many reasons, but mainly because people were starting to feel hurt after being told, "You are possessed." Because of this, many people that were new in the faith began leaving the church. It hurt me to know that we had failed them. Due to our lack of compassion, those people left the church without giving God or the church a chance because they did not understand why someone was judging them and telling them, "You have some demons in you and now we need to take them out." My heart fills with so much compassion as I write this.

This would also happen if the church's leadership did not agree with the person's lifestyle: they were automatically judged and commanded that they needed deliverance. All in all, lack of biblical truths and lack of proper biblical training were causing confusion and hurt in people's new walk with Christ.

But through this small group, the Lord had already begun doing something in my heart. He was about to heal a big wound. He was about to heal one of the biggest resentments I had toward that specific church. And He was about to unveil the shame that I had carried for so long for being part of that. I didn't know any better back then. But He is such a good Father, so faithful and kind to now walk me through healing and forgiveness toward myself, the church, and the leaders.

This small group was the initial step in breaking many false concepts about spiritual freedom. I needed this!

I decided to continue in this small group, as uncomfortable as it was going to get for me. I knew that in order to heal, I needed to take a risk, and joining this small group felt like a risk for me. I was exposing my heart to the possibility of getting hurt and offended again. But what if it wasn't a risk? What if this group of people would genuinely care for me and love me? Community is not always going to feel convenient. But if I wanted to heal, I knew I needed to take this step of faith. Stepping out in faith to speak about my pain, to get vulnerable with strangers—this is what "the truth shall set you free" meant for me. I had never talked about my pain and offense with others in the church, but something felt different about this group of women.

> Sometimes it takes a village to find healing.

Through community, we are able to find healing. In community, you start to see that the things you struggle with aren't your own battles, that you aren't the only one fighting. You are able to see God's grace, goodness, and sovereignty in the people around you, and it boosts your faith. The Bible encourages us to live a life of fellowship and unity with one another (Psalm 133:1).

Sometimes it takes a village to find healing. Ecclesiastes 4:12 (NLT) says, "A person standing alone can be attacked and defeated, but two can stand back-to-back and conquer. Three are even better, for a triple-braided cord is not easily broken."

It takes a special group of people, by your side, who are willing to carry you through the pain and hurt to find healing. I am pretty sure Jesus could have accomplished His purpose here on earth by Himself. He probably did not need the twelve. But here's the thing: even being God Himself, He knew that doing life with others was more impactful than doing it alone. If Jesus chose to do life with a special group of people, how much more should we? Jesus is the ultimate example of how we need to live our lives, and He never lived out His calling alone. Even on Jesus's last breath, He ministered to the man on the cross next to Him. Jesus was relational, never transactional. He understood the power of intentional community.

I have been a part of group counseling and individual counseling, and as much as I enjoy my individual monthly counseling sessions, nothing beats being in a room full of people who are ready to encourage you, lift you up, support you, pray for you, listen to you, and be there for you. I think we have over complicated community. Society makes us think that being a good friend or just being there for someone requires a lot. But in reality all we can do is be there for each other. All we need to do for someone else is have a listening ear and carry compassion on our sleeves and a box of tissues in our hand. The Lord will do the rest!

Apostle Peter was alone in prison, ready to be put on trial, when out of nowhere an angel woke him up and told him to get up, and his chains supernaturally fell off! You know why they fell off? Not because an angel showed up, but because Peter had a community, a church, that was praying for him! Community moves God to do the impossible! That is so good! Sometimes we are longing for a miracle, or we have big goals or dreams, but we don't even have a group of people praying for us. We have been told to keep our dreams to

> **Community moves God to do the impossible!**

ourselves because we can't trust the people around us. But I believe that's what the enemy wants! He doesn't want you connected to a group of people who are willing to stand in the gap for you and pray for you, for your God-given dreams. The enemy doesn't want you to find a community that is willing to support you and show you the love of Christ. So what does he do? He brings everything to destroy your need for other people and makes you think you can do it on your own. Truth is, none of us could ever outgrow community.

Here's the catch though: community and vulnerability are practically siblings. If we want to experience genuine community and profound healing, we have to open up.

Are any of you suffering hardships? You should pray. Are any of you happy? You should sing praises. Are any of you sick? You should call for the elders of the church to come and pray over you, anointing you with oil in the name of the Lord. Such a prayer offered in faith will heal the sick, and the Lord will make you well. And if you have committed any sins, you will be forgiven. Confess your sins to each other and pray for each other so that you may be healed. The earnest prayer of a righteous person has great power and produces wonderful results (James 5:13–16).

Vulnerability glorifies the Lord!

When we put ourselves in a state of vulnerability, we open room in our hearts for connection with other people. When we expose ourselves in vulnerability, we allow others to see our humanity, allowing that mask to fall off our spiritual and emotional selves and bringing all the focus to the goodness of God. Vulnerability glorifies the Lord! Vulnerability is not about us! It's about a good Father who sees beyond our mistakes, shortcomings, and weaknesses. It allows others to see the love, grace, and mercy of God over us.

I will never forget one of the most vulnerable moments of my life. I was in a meeting with some coworkers, when out of nowhere one of them began to share about how great her dad was and how she had grown up in a stable home with amazing parents. Suddenly, every emotion inside me was released from my body and crying out for help! I ran out of the office! I hid in the bathroom where two of my coworkers just sat there with me on that bathroom floor giving me tissues. (See why you gotta have that box of tissues handy?) You never know when someone is going to break down and let it all out.

My coworkers had no idea what I was going through until that day when I began to open up. It was so liberating! I finally understood what being vulnerable meant. I needed to stop hiding and shoving all these emotions inside of me. My dad had left my mom. I caught my dad cheating, and now my mom and little brother were homeless. I had carried that pain inside me for weeks, and I was hiding it, not letting it out to the Lord either. All my emotions came flooding out at a work meeting at an unexpected time. I had not intentionally sought out a time of community where I could open up and allow others to just sit there in my pain with me and pray for me. It was too painful to let it out, but so painful that it was eating me alive, until that very moment. That was the moment that I, for the first time ever, understood and felt the true meaning of His grace being sufficient for me!

> But he said to me, "My grace is sufficient for you, for my power is made perfect in weakness." Therefore I will boast all the more gladly about my weaknesses, so that Christ's power may rest on me (2 Corinthians 12:9).

I encourage you, my friend, to open up, let the walls down, and allow His power to be made perfect in your vulnerability. Don't let the stories of the power of our good Father go untold, others need to hear them too!

You know, for a long time I thought I had "my people," but one day I realized that I had outgrown them. I'd gotten married, I was a mom, and I had many other things on my plate. I was not able to even engage in certain conversations with them anymore; I was in a different stage of life. And that is okay, it happens! If you feel like that is what you are experiencing in this

I encourage you, my friend, to open up, let the walls down, and allow His power to be made perfect in your vulnerability. Don't let the stories of the power of our good Father go untold, others need to hear them too!

season, I encourage you to pray for friends, for a community that will bring you closer to the Lord. A community that will love you but also challenge you to grow and become the child of God He's called you to be.

A single mom at our church lost her home to lightning. The entire house caught on fire. The pictures were devastating. I could not believe this had happened to someone I knew! Someone who was part of my community had just lost their entire home, their belongings, their furniture, their clothes, their important documents—everything! I was the first one to get the call from our small group at church. My heart sank into my stomach as I heard, "Karina and her son are homeless. They lost their home in a fire!"

Within minutes our community had gotten a hotel room and clothing for them, meal trains, a GoFundMe account, and showers of prayers and so much love! As a community, we figured it out! All she had to do was call someone in her community! Community enables us to be vessels to pour out to others from a full cup. I'll tell you, it still warms my heart to know that the Lord used a group of people who were willing to lend a hand and help a single mom in need. These acts of kindness and the power of community impacted her so much that she later became the coordinator of an outreach ministry! Why? Because she was so inspired and touched by what God had done for her and her son through a community, she is now able to walk in her purpose and make a difference in the local community and church.

I have experienced this power of community myself. People have shown up to my door with flowers and food. They have sent handwritten cards and letters to encourage me, to remind me that I am not alone; they have created GoFundMe accounts and have even come to our home to clean for us while I was in a very dark season. I have tangibly felt the power of prayer carrying us through the toughest seasons of our lives.

I wasn't there to witness Peter's chains fall when he was in prison, but I have witnessed the power of those same prayers of a church united, praying for me and my family while we walked through grief and mourned for months. I am also a witness to the day Pastor JJ and Pastor Joey showed up to that hospital room when we were ready to disconnect my father-in-law from life support. They prayed for us,

Friend, don't run away from community anymore. Run to it!

they cried with us, they worshiped with us, and they embraced us. That is the power of community!

Friend, don't run away from community anymore. Run to it! Community is God's design for growth. We see it all over Acts 2. The Holy Spirit not only baptized the church, but He also brought people together. God's beautiful purpose for the church is for

The power of community is not something that someone told me about; it is something that has changed my heart, mindset, and spiritual walk, and it has allowed me to grow roots within the church.

people of different backgrounds, races, languages, and status to come together and do life in unity. Acts 2:42–47 teaches us that the people in the early church were devoted to one another, generous and sincere, and they shared meals together. Because of their intentionality to build community, the Lord added to their number daily! Meaning that genuine, intentional, and godly community attracts others to join Christ's family. This shows the world out there that we have a powerful God who can bring people together despite their differences in culture, upbringing, and experiences. We need more of that in and out of the church!

The power of community is not something that someone told me about; it is something that has changed my heart, mindset, and spiritual walk, and it has allowed me to grow roots within the church. I am a testimony of community in the church. Community was the medicine the doctor prescribed. The medicine worked, and I knew I needed to take it for the rest of my life to stay healthy.

Solitude in the Lord and community in the church were the tools the Lord used to bring me back to church.

Solitude in the Lord and community in the church were the tools the Lord used to bring me back to church. My heart was willing to be vulnerable. My mind was willing to shift. My body needed to step out of my comfort zone and go out of my way to seek and find a community. My emotions were willing to leave all pride, victimization, and wounds behind so that my whole being created space for the Holy Spirit to heal me!

Dear heavenly Father,

Thank You for Your grace, goodness, forgiveness, and healing! I pray that You would help me emotionally, physically, mentally, and spiritually find healing in this season. Help me find a godly and healthy community that only comes from You. I pray that You would open doors to new opportunities to seek and find community. I pray that my time in solitude with You begins to grow in this season. You know the desires of my heart, Lord, so I give them to You! I trust You, I praise You! I pray for Your peace, love, and grace to fill my heart at this moment. I sit here to spend time with You in solitude. Please speak to me, I want to hear Your voice. Use this time to heal me from any hurt, expose in me those things You want me to surrender to You. I pray that this time of solitude helps me continue to grow closer and deeper in You. In Jesus's name, amen.

CHAPTER 7

IT'S NOT ABOUT YOU

After being on the church-healed side and no longer on the church-hurt side, I've come to realize that most stories of church hurt have similar, if not the same, root of hurt: the wrong motives. I know, ouch! That is hard to hear. But I say this because once you heal, you realize that those things that hurt you initially were rooted in pride, either from the person or leader that hurt you or from yourself. I know that is also a hard pill to swallow. Here's the thing though: now that I have matured in a lot of ways in ministry, I do acknowledge that I walked myself into those hurtful moments. Which ones? The ones where I went to church because I was fearful I'd lose my position as an elder in the church. I was clearly serving out of fear. The ones where I pushed people to do things so my leadership would look good in front of the pastor. The ones where I said yes all the time to anything just to feed the "Meri does it all and can do it all" attitude.

Now I understand that none of that was pleasing to the Lord. Now I understand that the way I was serving was hurting me more than actually doing any good. Who's fault is that? Mine. I take ownership of the pain my own ego and pride caused myself and others. I say this now with all humbleness and confidence because I am healed, and now I understand that my motives are solely to please my heavenly Father.

SERVING

My heart was ready! Seven months after first attending Journey Church, I felt the Holy Spirit give me the green light to join a team and start serving in the church. Our pastor encouraged me to join the kids' team, but there was no way I wanted to serve with kids. I had just quit my teaching job to pursue our business full-time, and I was a brand-new mom trying to figure myself out. I remember saying to myself, "Kids ministry is not for me. I need to be doing something more important." Ha ha! Oh, trust me, that Meri was way too naive, and I'd even say prideful, to realize the process God wanted me to go through to fully embrace my healing.

So I joined the prayer team. It was convenient for me and the baby. I was comfortable and loved the people I served with. I was able to ease my way into it, and it helped me recognize that Journey Church was a safe place for community and genuine relationships. I knew that serving was the next step for me. Joining the prayer team was just the start of falling in love with serving. It filled me so much that I felt like maybe I wasn't doing enough for Jesus.

In reality though, are we ever doing enough for Jesus? He is so faithful and good, the least He deserves from us is a couple hours on Sundays to serve Him.

I served in the prayer team for a few weeks, and then I realized I also wanted to start helping out in the photography team. So I did. There wasn't much of a team yet, but people started noticing how much I loved it, and they started joining. I began to host workshops and editing tutorials so that others could learn and feel a sense of community and ownership in the team. I was absolutely loving my time with the team, and eventually we had seven other photographers who also enjoyed serving.

Serving in the photography team during that time was also part of my healing. I had no idea that it was until I looked back and realized everything the Lord had been teaching me. Different people with different backgrounds and ethnicities continued to join our church. This was great for me because it opened my eyes to what ministry should really look like.

Serving wasn't new for me. I grew up in church serving. I was at church seven days a week and spent hours serving. But I was serving my ego; I was serving for the acknowledgement of people. I was serving because that's what I *had* to do. That is what a good Christian does, right? They serve! But where was my heart? However, this time was different because my attitude was no longer that I have to serve but that I get to serve. Serving God and serving others is a ministry—the ministry of all of us in the church. Serving changed me! Serving has changed my heart for people, for ministry, and for leaders.

The year 2020 shook the world. It left a wound from which we are all still trying to heal. It allowed people to realize how much of a hustle mentality was consuming us and affecting our families. The pandemic isolated us socially and emotionally, and we are still feeling the effects on our worldwide economy. But there is one result of the 2020 world pandemic that is rarely mentioned: it stole some of the passion and urgency for people to serve in the local church.

I have connected with numerous church leaders and pastors who have shared their concerns toward the recent culture in our churches. The common theme is that people do not want to serve. They would rather stay home and watch church from there. I love that we can now stream church online, but what happens to the assignment that the Lord has given us to serve in the church? I believe the enemy is using isolation, fear, and lack of identity to separate us from the ultimate calling that the Lord has over our lives: to serve others. The enemy knows the power in the church when people come together to serve one another out of love, not selfish gains, and ultimately to serve the Lord.

> *It shall not be so among you. But whoever would be great among you must be your servant, and whoever would be first among you must be your slave, even as the Son of Man came not to be served but to serve, and to give his life as a ransom for many* (Matthew 20:26–28 ESV).

We live in a culture where everyone is hustling, trying to be successful, and looking for what benefits them. Phrases like "you do you, boo," which even I have said, are commonly used today. But is that what Jesus, God Himself came to do here on earth? Jesus came to serve, to give His life, to walk this earth with a posture of humility, wisdom, love, and sacrifice.

CHURCH IS FOR YOU!

I know it can be exciting to start serving in the local church, but before you jump in and decide to serve in a specific ministry, it's important to know and understand *why* you serve.

Some people jump into serving with the attitude of "Because y'all need the help!" Yes, the local church needs help to continue expanding the kingdom of God. But I also believe that the reason people grow tired of serving the Lord is because they've lost their sense of why. Every church has its mission statement, and it's important you believe in that mission so much that you are willing to invest your time, tithes, and gifts in it.

Knowing your why (the reason you want to serve in the local church) is essential to ensure that we serve the Lord with the right posture. Knowing your why keeps you focused on the mission you've decided to invest your time and gifts in. Knowing your why keeps you in the race when things get hard in your personal life. Knowing your why allows you to grow and get rooted in your relationship with the Lord. You serve because you are God's handiwork and you are created to do good works that God has already prepared for you to do. You serve because that's the example Jesus gave you. He said He did not come to be served but to serve and give his life as a ransom for many.

Serving with a why always in your mind and heart is so important. Being forced and shamed into serving is not healthy. Being asked to serve without knowing and having the why explained is very dangerous. It's dangerous for your

> **You serve because you are God's handiwork and you are created to do good works that God has already prepared for you to do.**

walk with God and it's dangerous for the church because you end up being frustrated and creating a toxic culture. Not knowing the why of the church and being in alignment with it is how you get hurt and grow resentful towards the local church and God.

As I said in the beginning of this book, we are going to be super vulnerable here. So here's a confession: the reason I am typing my life away about the importance of knowing our why is because I never understood my why. It was just something I did, and it had no profound meaning to my spiritual walk with the Lord. I was the perfect example of someone not knowing the why behind their service. But I knew I was tired, burnt out, and I rolled my eyes and put on the grouchiest face every time I had to serve, but I couldn't stop serving because it did not make sense to stop. So I started to create my own whys: for a title or a promotion, for my own ego, and for the validation of the people around me. But that was all pride and so far away from the heart of God.

The Lord had to take me through some dark rocky roads to understand the real why.

I learned that I am not that important. You are important in the eyes of the Lord, and we are all needed in the body of Christ. He has created you to impact the local church with your service, and He wants you to find your identity in Him as a child of God— not because of the title you hold or the seat you get to sit on during Sunday service. We don't serve because of our own merit. I needed that big reality check. I thought I was irreplaceable and no one could do what I did. So what did that do? It hurt myself and others. Because as much as you and I can contribute to the church, this is not about us! Serving is selfless! A good friend of mine once asked me who should be on top of the organizational chart in our church. Thankfully, she did not let me answer, and she immediately responded, "The souls!" That put everything into perspective for me. Another huge reality check. This is not about me, so why am I making it about me?

It's about the broken person walking through the doors of the church for the first time. It's about the person who's been through childhood trauma, the single mom who just needs a break, the widow who's lost the love of her life. Church is about the drug addict, the person with anger issues, the person giving God one last try before taking their own life. It's about the person crying out for love in silence and masking their pain and loneliness with social media followers. Church is for the child getting abused at home and bullied at school, the child with special needs, the child who lost a parent, the child who's surrounded by shame. Church is for the teenager battling with their self-worth and identity,

Church is for you, not about you!

the teenager trying to fit in at all costs, the teenager who's lost in a crowd of sin. The Church is for that marriage on the verge of divorce. Church is for the woman sleeping next to a man who abuses her. Church is for the man carrying anxiety and depression. Church is for the elderly sitting in loneliness six days out of the week. Church is for the leader with no sense of belonging or value. Church is for you, not about you!

What an honor it is to serve the broken, the lost, the ones the Lord holds dear. The ones Jesus died for. What a blessing it is to be the hands and feet of Jesus outside of the church. What a privilege it is to preach His love and truth through a simple smile and a warm welcome as you serve in the parking team. What a privilege it is to preach His love and truth through a gentle "Hello, welcome home," as you open the door. What a privilege it is to preach His love and truth by checking in families in Kids Ministry, teaching children the gospel, and planting a seed in the hearts of children that will forever remain. What a privilege it is to preach His love and truth by simply sitting with a teenager, listening to them, and telling them that they aren't alone, they are seen, and they are loved! What a privilege it is to preach His love and truth by leading people in worship, by holding a camera so that those who cannot physically attend church are still able to hear His Word. What a privilege it is to preach His love and truth by creating an environment that allows people to enjoy the experience of church. Those serving in production are not just putting lyrics on a screen and pushing buttons; they are creating a distraction-free environment that glorifies the Lord and allows people to lean into His presence. What a privilege it is to preach His love and truth by cleaning the house of the Lord or by using your administrative skills to have structure in the church. What a privilege it is to preach His love and truth as the body of Christ coming together to use our gifts for Him. My friend, you were created, saved, and called to serve God! What a privilege and honor it is to serve a God who is good, faithful, holy, almighty, wonderful, and beautiful.

My friend, you were created, saved, and called to serve God!

I encourage you to pray and ask God for forgiveness if you feel like your motives to serve in the church are not aligned with His will. Hey! No shame, okay? I was there before for a long time. He has redeemed me, healed me, and encountered me. He can and will do the same for you.

GOOD AND FAITHFUL SERVANT

I believe that the Lord wants to bring revival to the church, and this starts with faithful and loyal servants. There's a strong conviction in my heart that when I get to heaven, the Lord will not tell me, "Hey, Meri, good job being a wife," or "Good job being a mom," or "Good job writing that book," but He will tell me, "Good and faithful servant!" You see, nowadays everyone does something for the exchange

> **I believe that the Lord wants to bring revival to the church, and this starts with faithful and loyal servants.**

of another thing. Servanthood is not about that. Being a faithful servant means being a good steward of what the Lord has given us, at whatever capacity that looks like.

> *Again, it will be like a man going on a journey, who called his servants and entrusted his wealth to them. To one he gave five bags of gold, to another two bags, and to another one bag, each according to his ability. Then he went on his journey. The man who had received five bags of gold went at once and put his money to work and gained five bags more. So also, the one with two bags of gold gained two more. But the man who had received one bag went off, dug a hole in the ground and hid his master's money* (Matthew 25:14–18).

In the passage, "a man going on a journey," Jesus is sharing a parable most likely with His disciples. The man He is referring to is the master, and the servants are people that work for him. I believe Jesus wants to compare the master of the parable to our heavenly Father. He says that the master was going on a journey, meaning this man had places to go, things to do and accomplish. What is God's journey? Our heavenly Father is inviting us to walk this journey with Him. The one where we partner with Him, preach about Jesus, love people, serve one another, and essentially build and expand the kingdom of God. We are His people and He's called us to walk this with Him. He called! The Lord has called YOU, and not only that, but He has entrusted you with His wealth. What is His wealth? The gifts He has blessed you with.

When you think of your gifts as wealth, you receive a conviction that you hold something powerful and valuable. Maybe you look at your gift and think nothing of it, but God sees it differently. He doesn't only see you as the person who can hold the notes in the song, but He sees you as the one who will bring people closer to Jesus when you sing it. He doesn't only see you as the one who can make an argument, but as the one who will help His justice in the courtrooms. He doesn't only see you as the one who can negotiate, but He sees you as the one who will bring wealth to the kingdom of God to help plant churches all around the world. He doesn't only see you as a preschool teacher, but as a minister of the next generation who will bring revival. Friend, there is value in the gift that our Father has blessed you with.

In this same verse, there's an important message that we often overlook, and we have to pause and read it again: "Then he went on his journey." So the master gave the three servants his wealth and then left! What! Can you imagine? I don't know if I'd be able to give my servants this much wealth, which throughout this parable, a talent was worth about twenty years of a day laborer's wages. This means the master was really like, "Hey, I am giving you this, I trust you, it's super valuable," but then he left! I would have been micromanaging my wealth, giving special and specific instructions and keeping all these servants accountable. But God doesn't work that way! God trusts you, values you, loves you, and believes so much in you that He just wants you to draw near to Him and have a relationship with Him.

Let me explain "he went on his journey." I believe this is showing us a theme of responsibility in the master's absence. When Jesus shared this parable with His disciples, He was there with them, in person! But that wouldn't always be the case since one day Jesus would die, be resurrected, and go back to be with the Father. That doesn't mean He left us alone; that's why we have the Holy Spirit with us. This is His way of telling us that He will bless us with the gifts, but at the end of the day it is our free will to do what we want with them. Even though we do have free will with our gifts, the Lord wants us to use them for Him to expand His kingdom, worship Him, and bring them back to Him for His glory.

The parable continues in verses 19–25 by explaining what those servants did with the wealth. Two of them invested the wealth and the master said to each of them, "Well done, good and faithful servant! You have been faithful with a few things; I will put you in charge of many things. Come and share your master's happiness!" I have heard so many sermons that focus on the servants that did do something with the wealth. We praise them for their faithfulness and their great management skills. But have we ever stopped to think about the third servant? We shame him for being lazy and not producing more wealth.

Let's pause for a second and empathize with this servant. What was his reply when the master came back and asked what he did with the one gift?

> *Then the man who had received one bag of gold came. "Master," he said, "I knew that you are a hard man, harvesting where you have not sown and gathering where you have not scattered seed. So I was afraid and went out and hid your gold in the ground. See, here is what belongs to you* (Matthew 25:24–25).

There is so much to unpack here, mainly because for a long time, I was that one servant. I know I'm writing about how we should use our gifts for His kingdom and how serving is important, but if I could only count the many times I have felt like this servant. He was afraid! Afraid of what? Of messing it up! Here's the punch line: he did not think he was good enough to be a good steward of the master's wealth! If you are not crying, I am! Countless are the times I have felt inadequate, not ready, not good enough, not talented enough, not wise enough, not smart enough!

I remember walking to the stage to get ordained as a pastor and part of me physically could not do it. It was supposed to be such a special day and I could not fully enjoy that very special moment because I kept thinking, I am not ready for this; I am not equipped for this. How am I a pastor now? But those were just lies of the enemy! As I read the response of this servant, I wasn't picturing someone else—I saw myself!

In recent months I have learned that removing myself from the equation allows more space for the Holy Spirit to work through me, and that is enough! I do not need to have it all figured out to be the woman of God He has called me to be. I do not need the qualifications, education, race, experience, age, or even gender to qualify me. His grace qualifies me to do His will. He is not looking for degrees, a specific age, or your ability to do

His grace qualifies me to do His will.

something. He is looking for a servant who is ready to be obedient and available to His call—someone to simply say yes to Him. He is looking for someone who will seek Him first and above anything else. He is looking for a heart that is willing to serve Him. God is calling you out and asking you to stop hiding, to stop overthinking, and to remove yourself from the equation. He is looking for risk-takers who will grab His wealth and multiply it.

Don't you think the other two servants were also afraid? I wonder if the difference between the two servants who invested their wealth and the one who didn't was that the other two servants had a closer relationship with the master. Maybe they knew what the master wanted them to do with it and that he had a reward for them. But they would have only known that if they had a relationship with him.

Friend, do not let feelings of inadequacy tell you otherwise! The enemy can't change what God thinks about you, but he can change what you think of yourself. He can get in your thoughts and stop you from living in the fullness of the calling the Lord has for you.

I have recently learned that inadequacy is rooted in pride. The enemy

Serving is selfless!

masks our pride with false humility. Thoughts like I'm not good enough aren't from God, and they aren't rooted in humbleness; they're rooted in our inability to see ourselves how our heavenly Father sees us. You know what truly disqualifies us? Pride. Ouch! I know that hurts. It hurt me then because I had walked through years of feeling inadequate until I learned to surrender. I've learned that the only way to truly surrender this pride is by getting to know my Father through His Word, through prayer, and through solitude. I allow the Holy Spirit to speak into the person God has created me to be rather than how I view myself. I allow room for thoughts that come from Him. I allow my identity to come from Him and not from the hurt I was once marked with.

I allowed my Father, my creator, to heal my wounds and my shortcomings from the hurt I've experienced within and outside of the church. I have allowed the hurt I once experienced to be the one thing that brings me closer to Jesus. I've heard that there is beauty in pain. I know that the pain that once was inside me is now a beautiful story that the Lord has used to mold me to His unique design.

I was there once, and as much as I empathize with that servant, I could no longer allow fear to paralyze me. I had to do something

Friend, do not let feelings of inadequacy tell you otherwise! The enemy can't change what God thinks about you, but he can change what you think of yourself. He can get in your thoughts and stop you from living in the fullness of the calling the Lord has for you.

about it. I surrendered and allowed the Lord to mold me, prune me, and shape me. I allowed Him to renew my thoughts about myself. It was not an easy process, but I have seen the great fruit out of it.

I encourage you to pray if you relate to this servant, perhaps you have not been a good steward of the wealth He has entrusted to you.

THE MOST BEAUTIFUL EXAMPLE OF SERVANTHOOD

When Jesus bent down to wash His disciples' feet, He did not remove their brand-new white Nike sneakers and clean socks. Back in Jesus's day people wore sandals, they walked everywhere, and the streets were made out of dirt. So you can just imagine the way their feet looked. He took off their dirty, nasty, dusty sandals. If you hate feet, I apologize for the visual description. But I want you to transport your imagination to that very moment when Jesus washed the feet of his disciples. This was not just a simple act of washing feet. It was the ultimate example of servanthood.

The Word says that Jesus took off His outer clothing and wrapped a towel around His waist. This act of servanthood was vulnerable, holy, and humble. He washed their feet and dried them with the towel wrapped around His waist. When we forgive and serve, our hearts are surrendered, and our posture cares more about what God will do than what we care or think about ourselves.

You know what is wild to me? That Jesus not only picked Judas as one of His disciples, but He also washed Judas's feet knowing that it was in his heart to betray Him. And Jesus washed Peter's feet knowing that he would deny Him three times. I know we tend to pick on Peter for having a temper and overreacting, but can we be real? We can be like Peter at times. In our walk, we can be all sold out for Jesus, but as soon as trouble shakes us, we are quick to forget His goodness, making our soul unconsciously deny His fatherhood over us. But there is something that I love about Peter: he was teachable. The man had so many questions and comments; he makes me laugh, mainly because sometimes I have Peter moments. We later learn that Peter repented of his ways and allowed Jesus's love to embrace him because an encounter with the Holy Spirit transformed him.

Washing the feet of others was the lowest of the low. Jesus was not afraid to get on His knees and dirty His hands to serve those He loved and those He knew would betray and deny Him. Jesus washed their dirty feet knowing His authority came from God, and that made Him humble. Humility is the willingness to go to the places and do the things no one else wants to do because it doesn't look or feel glorious.

After He washed their feet, put on His outer garments, and resumed His place, He said to them, "Do you understand what I have done to you? You call me 'Teacher' and 'Lord,' and you are right, for so I am. If I then, your Lord and Teacher, have washed your feet, you also ought to wash one another's feet" (John 13:12–14 ESV).

How many times has the Lord asked us to serve someone or to serve in the church, but because it's inconvenient or doesn't look pleasing or isn't on a platform, or because we don't like someone in the church or someone said something that offended us, we are quick to say no or to decline that planning center request? No, this is not to shame you or make you want

> **Humility is the willingness to go to the places and do the things no one else wants to do because it doesn't look or feel glorious.**

to accept to serve out of guilt. But for real? Let's take a moment to examine our heart, soul, and mind. Because Jesus didn't even think twice about getting on His knees, taking off His clothing, being uncomfortable, and washing the feet of people that were once tax collectors and greedy, prideful thieves. They weren't worthy of His servanthood. They weren't worthy of His sacrifice and neither are we.

But Jesus still did it! He knew it would make a difference in their lives, in our lives, and for generations to come. And that's exactly what He wants to do through your servanthood. He wants to make a difference in you, through you, for the people around you, and the people you don't even know. There is power in that YES to serve Him! Step out of your comfort zone and step into the fullness of the perfect will He has for you!

Dear heavenly Father,

I recognized that there have been seasons where I have made serving about myself. I pray that as you continue to heal me, you transform my heart to a servant heart. Help me step out in faith and out of my comfort zone to serve You and do what you have called me to do. I pray you give me the zeal to serve You with love and passion. Help me steward well the gifts that you have given me. In Jesus's name, amen.

Here's the problem I've encountered in the church: when we make it about anything other than the Gospel of Jesus, we make it about ourselves and what's in it for us and that's when we begin to have massive problems in the church.

CHAPTER 8

AN ONGOING JOURNEY

I wish I could end this book by saying, *my friend, if you stay in the church and you do everything right, I promise you that you will never get hurt again.* Well, I'd be lying to you. So, we're going to continue the theme of honesty and vulnerability in this book. Truth is, you are going to experience things in the church that will probably offend you, rub you a certain way, or you will simply not agree with. Some things will hurt you, even in a healthy church. I've been writing this book for over a year now and I am confident that the Lord slowed down the process so that I could experience a few other things that have created frustrations in me within the church.

The issues we encounter in the church, whether past, present, or future aren't new to God. There were many problems in the early churches too. In the first letter of Corinthians the Apostle Paul reminds the church that the Gospel is what unites the church. Here's the problem I've encountered in the church: when we make it about anything other than the Gospel of Jesus, we make it about

As you step up to
serve and to lead,
you have to stay
alert that your
heart remains
humble and after
God's own heart
and that you
always do ministry
with the posture
of loving God and
loving people.

ourselves and what's in it for us and that's when we begin to have massive problems in the church. At that point we're no longer making it about loving God and loving people. We have to be alert and on guard of where our hearts are as we serve and as we step into leadership in the church so that we never make it about ourselves. In this very exact season in my journey in ministry the Lord continues to teach me to have a soft heart as I face situations within the church.

King David was recognized for being a man after God's own heart, yet he did not always get it right. There were many moments in his leadership where he failed morally and before he took his last breath, he told Solomon to kill all his enemies. David died with murder and revenge in his heart. David let his heart get hardened. Truth is, even great leaders aren't right all the time. It's not just about facing trials, it's about remaining pure even when we go astray. Ministry is not always going to be a walk in the park. We are going to face hard times, but will you let those issues in the church harden your heart towards serving Him and stepping into the calling He has for you? Friend, you are going to see leaders not always get it right. You are not always going to get it right either. As you step up to serve and to lead, you have to stay alert that your heart remains humble and after God's own heart and that you always do ministry with the posture of loving God and loving people.

I believe that God wants us to look at the Apostle Paul and Apostle Peter not only for what they did for and in the early church but for their resilience to continue showing up, preaching the Gospel while being persecuted by people in the church. They remained faithful and obedient to God's perfect will even when the church rejected them, even when they saw things in the church that weren't pleasing to the Lord. God used them as a voice in the church to bring order. They remained faithful to the call. I believe that's exactly what the Lord does through us as we remain healthy and with the right heart posture. He wants to use your testimony of what you have endured in the church to bring others to a place of healing.

IDENTIFYING A HEALTHY CHURCH

I have good news, my friend, that even though, no, we will never have the perfect church, we can build *healthy* churches! Healthy churches will only be possible if we focus on our personal growth with our heavenly Father. A healthy church is one who is willing to go through the pruning, cutting, the shaping, the digging to expose those things in our hearts that are not pleasing to Him. A healthy church is one that has its identity in Christ, one whose confidence is in Him not in man. A healthy church is resilient to the trials.

> **Healthy churches will only be possible if we focus on our personal growth with our heavenly Father.**

One who is willing to stand firm and remain! Healthy churches start with individuals who are willing to go through the healing so that others may heal too.

Oftentimes people who are going through difficult seasons in the church ask me "how do I know God is asking me to leave or stay in the church?" A friend shared an illustration with me that I think is helpful to answer this question. "Is the ground shaking or are you shaking?" If God is your foundation and you are standing on Him, there are going to be moments where He asks you to move. If He is calling you to move you are going to feel the ground move below you. Other times you are going to be scared and your heart and your mind are going to want to keep you from staying planted in the place God is asking you to be. So how do you know if the church you are looking at is the right place for you? First you pray, and you remain in Him. Next you look for signs that the church is healthy.

HEALTHY CHURCHES LOVE PEOPLE

I remember a time I really started to see that Journey Church was healthy and not like the culture I was coming from. There was a woman who joined the photography team that was married to another woman. On the day I found this out, I thought, Wait—someone homosexual comes to our church? I was shook! This moment brought me back to the day a homosexual walked into the previous church we attended, where they were judged, asked to repent, and told not to come back to the church until they were not in sin anymore. How hurtful is that? I asked myself how Jesus would have handled that?

Part of me wrestled to understand my position as a woman of God, a believer, and a church leader. How should I treat her? Do I say anything about her lifestyle? I let the Holy Spirit bring peace and wisdom in that moment.

This moment was freeing for me because I realized we were doing church right! People who are lost are really coming to our church wanting to be part of a community and to get plugged in! At that very moment I understood the true meaning of before you believe, you belong! Granted, there are guidelines in our church to make sure that we are caring and walking with them with wisdom, love, and compassion. But it is not our duty to push them away or to push change into their lives. It is our responsibility to teach them what the Bible says about their lifestyle and allow the Lord to use time and community to heal and transform their lives.

Healthy churches walk people through sanctification, allowing the Holy Spirit and their example of a righteous life to be what inspires the change in a person.

Jesus confronted the experts of the Law and loved the lost. He unconditionally loved those who were broken, sick, condemned, and oppressed. That is what we do as the church: we love on them and allow the Holy Spirit and the Word of the Lord to transform their addictions, ways of the world, sins, and identities. I have been blessed to witness the transformation the Holy Spirit has done in the lives of many who have stepped in a church filled with love and grace.

Unhealthy churches pray for people to find healing and freedom, but then close the doors because they don't look like them. They pray for people to repent from their ways, but then close the doors by judging them and not loving them how God loves them.

Healthy churches understand that loving the "sinner" does not mean loving their sin. We sin too! We are all sinners, and just because our sin looks less sinful, it does not mean we should close the doors of our church to those that are hurting and in bondage. Healthy churches walk people through sanctification, allowing the Holy Spirit and their example of a righteous life to be what inspires the change in a person.

HEALTHY CHURCHES HAVE HEALTHY LEADERSHIP

A healthy church starts with healthy leadership. Healed people help people heal, healthy churches are full of people who are healed so they can be a healing place for others. How do we know when there's healthy leadership in a church? When the church is growing not just in numbers, but the people in it, starting with the staff and leaders, are growing as disciples of Jesus, producing good fruit in their marriages, homes, and ministries. We know it is healthy when the church is walking in unity and in the fullness of God.

> **A healthy church starts with healthy leadership. Healed people help people heal.**

In Ephesians 4, the apostle Paul teaches us how to be a healthy church. A church that is humble, gentle, patient, kind, compassionate, and one that bears with one another in love, honors one another, and forgives one another as Christ forgave us. A body that walks in unity in faith, one that is mature and attains the whole measure of the fullness of Christ. A church whose head is Christ and the whole body is "held together by every supported ligament, grows and builds itself up in love, as each part does its work" (v. 16).

That's the church, y'all! A body united so that the leadership can equip its people for works of service to simply make Jesus known! Why do we make it about anything other than Christ Himself? It was Jesus's idea to build the church in the first place—not ours.

HEALTHY CHURCHES BUILD PEOPLE

The Lord has used ministry to transform and renew my heart. God can use anything to shape us as long as we let Him. But He wanted me to understand that we need to use ministry to build people; we don't use people to build ministry. I never realized that a lot of my hurt came from feeling used by leaders. For a long time I thought that people were the tools that God uses to build His church. But no, I had it twisted! God uses the ministry He has for us to build our faith, to bring us closer to Him, to mold us, to shape us, to prune us, and to know who we are in Him! If we use people to build the church, then that's when people start to feel used, unappreciated, burnt out, and more like a tool rather than a child of God.

> We need to use ministry to build people; we don't use people to build ministry.

How do we care for the people first? We understand that they have free will. We don't force people to serve or to do something in the church that is not their passion. We see them as God's children, not for their titles or abilities. We see them for who God created them to be, not for their talents. We don't ask what they can do for the church; we ask what the church can do for them. We first care about them as people before we start asking them for a commitment. We pray for them, we care for them, we spend time with them, we build a genuine relationship with them, we walk with them through hard times, we love them, we celebrate with them, and we simply serve them.

That's what Jesus did! Again, He's our ultimate example of a healthy leader. Jesus was relational, never transactional. Jesus cared more about His disciples' hearts. He didn't see them for their way of life, talents, or knowledge. If Jesus cared about that, He would have chosen the experts of the Law to be His disciples, but He didn't. He picked those that He knew needed the love of a good God: people He could pour into and who needed to walk alongside Him to experience real-life transformation.

> **We don't ask what they can do for the church; we ask what the church can do for them.**

Jesus first walked with His disciples, He first built friendships with them, He served them before asking anything from them, and He loved them first!

THE CALL TO LEADERSHIP

I was very happy and comfortable being a stay-at-home mom, working on our business, and serving in the photo team at church. Life was great! Then, out of nowhere one day, I got a call from our pastor asking, "Meri, would you like to apply for our Kids Director position?" Who? Me? Nah! Thanks, but no . . . I asked Martin, "Why me?" He said, "Why not you, babe?" You would think I'd be humbled by the question, but nope! I was just full of pride. I thought I was way too good for Kids Ministry. But what I didn't know was that what I needed to soften this stubborn heart was Kids Ministry.

My initial answer was no, but I still went home and prayed about it. The Lord reminded me of a youth conference I had attended

God wanted to show me that a healthy church starts with me! He wanted me to understand that the body of Christ cannot function at its full potential without a healthy heart.

when I was sixteen years old where I told God, "I will go where You send me. You have my yes, God!" Well, this time He was asking me to go somewhere I did not want to go. He was asking me to step out of my comfort zone, move where the foundation was moving to, and I needed the faith to keep my eyes on Him and to trust Him. I knew I was stepping into a healthy church and that allowed me to say yes.

A few months later, I joined the Journey Church staff family. I walked in with lots of insecurities, self-doubt, lack of confidence, and so many questions (like why me?). My first day on the job I felt out of place, thinking this was not for me. I was surrounded by five incredible leaders who seemed like they knew what they were doing, full of experience, and I was the newbie. Of course, they all welcomed me with open arms and big smiles. They weren't the issue—I was. My insecurities made me feel out of place. Do I even belong at this table?

Pastor JJ pulled me aside one of the first days of working at church and asked me, "Meri, are you healed? If you're not, it's okay. I just want to make sure you continue to heal." I said, "Yes, I am ninety percent there!" And I was healing, but there were still some wounds within me that the Lord wanted to completely heal. God wanted to show me that a healthy church starts with me! He wanted me to understand that the body of Christ cannot function at its full potential without a healthy heart. My heart still needed pruning.

It appears that God picks people who seem the least qualified through human eyes. God looks for someone with an obedient servant's heart, someone willing to be pruned and molded by Him. That's all He cares about. That's what He did with me. He did not care if I had done this before or if I had the qualifications or experience. He wanted to continue molding me, and He used ministry for that purpose.

He wanted to show me that a healthy church is possible. He wanted to show me what He could do with a simple yes! Even though that yes did not feel simple for me. I can't imagine what my life would be like now without that yes! The Lord has used ministry to mold me, prune me, humble me, and show me that this in fact is not about me.

The Lord used ministry to transform my identity as a daughter of God and to transform my bitter heart into a soft heart that hurts when others hurt. He has used ministry to transform my offenses into forgiveness and to transform my confidence into Godfidence. I am so grateful for that, and I wouldn't change anything about it.

The Lord has used ministry to mold me, prune me, humble me, and show me that this in fact is not about me.

HEALTHY LEADERSHIP QUALITIES

Putting away my degree and saying yes to being in full-time ministry was never one of my life goals. I never joined an internship program at a church to help me grow in ministry. Oh boy, I wish I did, though.

Full-time ministry is being the hands and feet of Jesus wherever we go.

Becoming a pastor was never something I dreamed of as a little girl. Not even serving in the church had motivated anything in me to one day want to be in full-time ministry in the church. I say "full-time ministry in the church" because full-time ministry looks different for everyone, but it has the same common goal. Full-time ministry can mean being a mom, dad, doctor, a nurse, a teacher, a businessperson, an architect, an accountant, a dentist, or an employee in a corporate setting; full-time ministry is being the hands and feet of Jesus wherever we go. He asked us to make disciples of all nations.

The world doesn't need another pastor behind a pulpit; the world needs children of God who are willing and available to make His name known in and out of the church. We need to bring the sick, the broken, the rejected, and the lost to the feet of Christ. Jesus was the church on foot! We follow His example.

Full-time ministry is living for our Father and doing everything for His glory!

Why does it matter if I preach fire on a Sunday but mistreat people at the grocery store? Full-time ministry is living for our Father and doing everything for His glory! It's making disciples at our jobs, at schools, at grocery stores, anywhere we go! Full-time ministry is simply loving God and loving people.

Just because someone carries the title of a leader doesn't inherently qualify them as a healthy one. Adolf Hitler, for instance, possessed qualities commonly associated with leadership – vision, strategy, and influence – yet he was far from being a healthy leader. Despite his ability to mobilize followers, his leadership was toxic, characterized by hatred and manipulation. It's crucial to recognize that leadership isn't solely about holding a title but rather about embodying the right values and intentions. Had Hitler possessed a compassionate and ethical approach, he could have been considered a healthy leader. It is important to understand that it is not about having the title of a leader but about having the right posture to be a healthy leader when God calls us to step into that role in the church.

HEALTHY LEADERS GUARD THEIR HEARTS

Rejoice in the Lord always. I will say it again: Rejoice! Let your gentleness be evident to all. The Lord is near. Do not be anxious about anything, but in every situation, by prayer and petition, with thanksgiving, present your requests to God. And the peace of God, which transcends all understanding, will guard your hearts and your minds in Christ Jesus (Philippians 4:4-7).

One of the purposes why Paul wrote this letter to the church in Philippi was to encourage believers to remain joyful in affliction, united in service and to stand firm in Christ. When Paul wrote this he was in prison for preaching the gospel. Yet, he tells us to rejoice, to be gentle, to not be anxious, and to pray. Paul reminds us to pray because that is the weapon that will guard your heart from the hurt of growing into deeper wounds. God wants to hear what is frustrating you, He wants to know how you feel, He wants to carry you through that difficult situation. But we have to invite Him in. When prayer is our first response to issues, the Lord will fill our hearts with peace. A peace that does not make sense. A peace that will guard your heart and mind. We claim to want world peace, but how can we when we don't carry inner peace? We want love to rule the world, but we don't let the love of a good Father rule our hearts. One of the most effective ways to guard our hearts is by filling it with the truth of God's Word. Psalms 119:11 says, "I have

> We claim to want world peace, but how can we when we don't carry inner peace? We want love to rule the world, but we don't let the love of a good Father rule our hearts.

It is important to understand that it is not about having the title of a leader but about having the right posture to be a healthy leader when God calls us to step into that role in the church.

hidden your word in my heart that I might not sin against you."
When we saturate our hearts and minds with Scripture, we are
equipping ourselves to discern between what is good and what is
harmful. But guarding our hearts isn't just about keeping out the
bad; it's also about cultivating the good. We should actively seek to
fill our hearts with love, joy, peace, patience, kindness, goodness,
faithfulness, gentleness, and self-control—the fruit of the Spirit
(Galatians 5:22-23).

It is important to guard our hearts as we face difficult situations in the church so that our hearts do not harden. The LORD
says, "Don't harden your hearts as Israel did at Meribah, as they
did at Massah in the wilderness. For there your ancestors tested
and tried my patience, even though they saw everything I did. For
forty years I was angry with them, and I said, 'They are people
whose hearts turn away from me. They refuse to do what I tell
them.' So in my anger I took an
oath: 'They will never enter my
place of rest'" (Psalms 95:8-11).

It is important to guard our hearts as we face difficult situations in the church so that our hearts do not harden.

Here, the Lord is reminding
us not to harden our hearts as the
Israelites did. They turned away
from God due to the hardships
they faced. The Lord used these
verses to remind me that while
I remain in the church, I must
not allow difficult situations to
harden my heart. If we continue to harbor unforgiveness, hurt, and
offenses in the church, we won't be able to enter a place of peace
as we serve the Lord. He desires for us to be in the church with
hearts filled with His love, grace, and mercy. Let's not be leaders
with hardened hearts, seeking influence but neglecting an intimate
relationship with the Father.

HEALTHY LEADERS RESPOND DIFFERENTLY

I have found myself in recent situations that have caused some hurt in me within the church. But the way I've responded to the hurt has been completely different than how I once reacted to the hurt. I am able to respond with it from a place of forgiveness, grace, love, compassion, and confidence as a Child of God.

Responding does not mean running away from the situation, or avoiding the issue, or not confronting the issue. Responding is being in the midst of the chaos, seeing the things that are wrong, but not allowing bitterness to grow roots in your heart. It's okay to feel the emotions, the frustrations, Jesus felt them too. Jesus flipped tables when He went to Jerusalem and saw the way the people were dishonoring God's temple. He said, "Get these out of here! Stop turning my Father's house into a market!" (John 2:16). I am not saying go flip tables at your church, trust me I know the feeling of wanting to do that too... but it is okay to have a zeal for wanting to be a healthy church. However, I've had to learn how to respond so that I don't actually flip the tables and end up in jail.

Healthy leaders respond, they don't react. Stepping into leadership in the church has taught me the difference between reacting and responding. Reacting is automatic and driven by emotions, while responding is more intentional, reflective, and considers both the present moment and the future implications. Developing the ability to respond rather than react is often associated with greater emotional intelligence and interpersonal effectiveness. Responding requires emotional maturity, self awareness, and resilience from the leader. Healthy leaders are often emotionally intelligent, meaning they can recognize, understand, and manage their own emotions. Healthy leaders have a deep understanding of themselves, including their strengths, weaknesses, values, and triggers. This self-awareness enables them to recognize when they are being triggered or reactive and take steps to regulate their emotions before responding. Resilience is the ability to bounce back from setbacks and challenges. Healthy leaders possess a high level of resilience, allowing them to maintain composure and perspective in difficult situations. God wants to build churches with healthy leaders who are

Developing the ability to respond rather than react is often associated with greater emotional intelligence and interpersonal effectiveness.

going to respond when issues arise so that we handle conflicts in a healthy way. Remember, we will never be able to please everyone. Jesus was perfect, yet He was crucified. When He felt the betrayal and the weight of sin, He still chose to do God's perfect will.

HEALTHY LEADERS HAVE HEALTHY CONFLICT

Recently I experienced a situation in the church that I felt was not fair, and felt the decisions our leadership was making did not make sense. I experienced frustration, anger, and felt hurt about comments and decisions being made. I responded with forgiveness and I ran to prayer! I asked the Lord to bring peace into my heart and my mind. I brought my heart to a place of gratitude, and asked the Lord to take control of the situation. The Lord began to open doors for me to be able to speak up and bring unhealthy things to the light in the organization. As much as I cried and experienced hurt, my heart was in the right place. My heart just wanted God's perfect will. The motives of my heart weren't to prove myself right, I was fighting from wisdom, grace, and love for a healthy church.

Being in ministry and working alongside people has shaped my heart into not jumping into conclusions and creating my own narratives out of the situation. That has been the secret to guarding my own heart. When we create our own narratives out of the situation, we don't allow the Holy Spirit to take full control of the situation, and we react out of hurt. I love how Jesus called out the situations that weren't aligned to God's will in such a gracious way. John eight tells the account of when Jesus was teaching, when the Pharisees approached Him with a woman caught in the act of adultery. She deserved to be stoned, according to the Law. The Pharisees asked Jesus, "What do you say?" They did not ask with the intention of getting His input—they didn't care about that. Their hearts were so far away from grace, love, and God that they missed God Himself! When our hearts aren't guarded, we walk around just trying to prove ourselves right, we stop being the light in situations and worst of all, we miss God Himself. Instead of bringing peace and grace, we bring more hurt and condemnation to the body of Christ.

The negative narratives don't allow us to surrender to the Lord and be at peace that all things will work together for our good.

Jesus carried that out with so much wisdom, knowing that talking to the woman while those people were there would do no good; He did not rush to find judgment in her. He was giving space for the right moment to speak to her. He took His time to carefully handle the situation. Jesus handled this with so much grace, love, compassion, and forgiveness. Imagine if we handled all issues within the church, or outside the church, with wisdom, grace, love, and compassion. He simply said, "Let him who is without sin among you be the first to throw a stone at her." He was like, "Y'all need to check yourselves." Before we start accusing or letting pride creep into our hearts, let's check ourselves!

The truth is, sometimes our motives or own truths aren't aligned with truth and love either. I like to say there's three sides to every story. Your perspective, their perspective, and the truth. So we need to check our hearts and ask ourselves, Am I assuming the best in them? Give space for the Holy Spirit to scan your heart, and allow Him to work in you. I believe that is exactly the example Jesus wants us to follow when we face situations that are going to potentially hurt us. That yes, we can assume the best in a

My friend, your story of pain carries purpose, and He wants to use it for His glory and His kingdom.

person to protect our hearts, but we still need to have the conversations to ensure there's no room left for negative narratives. Negative narratives hurt the church. It's leaving the door open for thoughts that aren't godly towards the other person or the situation. The negative narratives don't allow us to surrender to the Lord and be at peace that all things will work together for our good. When a situation arises, don't jump into conclusions that will cause more hurt. Instead believe that the Lord is at work in the situation and have the conversations you need to have to find clarity in the situation and express the hurt you felt. Jesus did not focus on condemning the women, He comforted the Pharisees in such a wise and peaceful way. He cared about bringing peace at that moment. Jesus shows us that when we assume the best, we extend grace and forgiveness, and even acknowledge the potential for change and growth in every person. Assuming the best protects our hearts from offense, unforgiveness, and rage against one another. Assuming the best exhibits the power of redemption, encouraging us to look beyond people's mistakes and to love them as God loves them.

My friend, your story of pain carries purpose, and He wants to use it for His glory and His kingdom. God uses broken people to fulfill His perfect will. I firmly believe that He desires for you to seek healing because there's even greater purpose in your story when you heal. Remember, the hurt is not your fault, but it is your responsibility to decide what to do with the pain.

Are you willing to go through the pruning to heal?

Are you willing to take that step of forgiveness?

Are you willing to love God with all your heart, mind, and soul?

Are you willing to love the church regardless of its imperfections?

Are you willing to remain pure-hearted and resilient through the trials?

Are you willing to use your story of pain to help others find healing?

Are you willing to heal?

A healthy church starts with healed people.

It starts with me.

And it starts with you.

Dear heavenly Father,

Thank You for bringing me this far into my healing journey. Thank You for speaking to me. Thank You for pruning me. I thank You for redeeming me, for forgiving me, for loving me, and for having grace over me. Help me love Your church even with its imperfections! Give me the zeal to remain healthy so I can help build a healthy church. Help me walk others into healing as You have walked me through it. **Because healed people, help people heal!** *I love You so much, Father! In Jesus's name, amen.*

A healthy church starts with healed people. It starts with me. And it starts with you.

ACKNOWLEDGMENTS

There are certain people in life who, from the moment you meet them, you feel their love embrace you, and for me that is Pastors JJ and Liz. Thank you both for your unconditional love to my family and me. Thank you for being part of my healing journey. Thank you for always assuming the best in Martin and me. Thank you for seeing the calling and anointing over our lives. Thank you for guiding us and caring for us in the worst and most painful moments of our lives. I am eternally grateful for all the leadership advice, training, and wisdom you both have imparted on me.

I am a firm believer that God knew I needed a leader, pastor, and friend like Pastor Joey.

Joey, thank you for being a leader who genuinely loves people. Thank you for showing me what being an intentional leader looks like. I am grateful for the way you have supported me through the process of writing this book, for being the first person to read it. Thank you for believing in me from the moment we met. I can say I am the leader that I am today because of the way you have believed in me. Thank you for being part of my healing journey and teaching me how to be the pastor I am today. I appreciate your leadership more than you'll ever know.

God placed a special group of people in my life to give me another chance to be a healthy leader. Thank you, Journey Kids team and leadership, for giving me the opportunity to walk alongside you all. Thank you to all the coordinators: Ali, Angelina, Brittany, Cristina, Emily, Kassandra, Krystal, Priscilla, Steph, Vanessa, and Vianca who have walked this incredible journey with me. Thank you for believing in me, for loving me, for all the memories we've built together. Thank you for allowing me to pour into you all. I am humbled to be part of your walk with the Lord. Thank you for your endless prayers and for helping me build a healthy and genuine community in our church.

Thank you to my dear friend, Rachel for believing in me and in the impact this book will make. Thank you for spending hours and hours helping me perfect this God given book. Thank you for your listening ear, for the endless laughs, and for your genuine support and love. I am so blessed by your sweet friendship.

AUTHOR BIO

Meri Duarte – a devoted wife, mother of two boys, entrepreneur, and pastor, finds her greatest joy in serving Jesus. With a degree in Psychology and Bible Studies, she aims to deepen others' understanding of God and strengthen their faith journey. Meri's unwavering commitment to God extends to writing and preaching His Word, fostering spiritual growth, empowering others, and developing strong leaders within the church. She is a social butterfly who cherishes friendships and cultivates connections with others. Currently, she serves as a Pastor in Orlando, FL.

Made in the USA
Columbia, SC
07 February 2025

52565740R00100